REIMAGINING

— *Our* —

AMERICAN REPUBLIC

A COMMONSENSE VISION
FOR UNCOMMON TIMES

PETER W. FREY

GREENLEAF
BOOK GROUP PRESS

Published by Greenleaf Book Group Press
Austin, Texas
www.gbgpress.com

Distributed by Greenleaf Book Group

For ordering information or special discounts for bulk purchases, please contact Greenleaf Book Group at PO Box 91869, Austin, TX 78709, 512.891.6100.

Design and composition by Greenleaf Book Group
Cover design by Greenleaf Book Group and Sheila Parr
Cover image © iStockphoto / yamonstro

Publisher's Cataloging-in-Publication data is available.

Print ISBN: 978-1-62634-602-4

eBook ISBN: 978-1-62634-603-1

Part of the Tree Neutral® program, which offsets the number of trees consumed in the production and printing of this book by taking proactive steps, such as planting trees in direct proportion to the number of trees used: www.treeneutral.com

TreeNeutral®

Printed in the United States of America on acid-free paper

18 19 20 21 22 23   10 9 8 7 6 5 4 3 2 1

First Edition

DEDICATION

As the twig is bent so grows the tree. My sixth-grade teacher, Mrs. Manikowski, took me under her wing and provided an introduction to intellectual endeavor that has stayed with me for life. In high school, Kenneth Fielding taught chemistry and physics, imparting to me a love for science that led to my college academic focus. At Yale, professors Fred Sheffield, Allan Wagner, and Neal Miller converted a young man with many rough edges into a budding young scientist. In graduate school at the University of Wisconsin, Leonard Ross, my major professor, contributed hours and hours of his valuable time working to improve my writing skills. My master's thesis went through thirteen revisions before submission to the review committee. I am indebted to these individuals, as well as many others, who provided valuable advice and encouragement that indelibly altered my life.

In my freshman year of college, I met a lovely young lady who has enriched and ordered my life. After graduation, we recited our marriage vows to live together from this day forward—for better, for worse, for richer, for poorer, in sickness and in health, until death do us part. Fifty-four years later, we can look back on the joys of many little victories, several very serious crises, and the love and companionship that make life worth living. I dedicate this book to my wife, Ruth, and to the educators who generously invested in my future.

CONTENTS

PREFACE

Growing up in the 1940s and 1950s, I experienced a world that is vastly different from the world experienced by young people today. The contrast is stark. There were no home computers or cell phones. No one had even imagined being able to access information from something like the internet. I was a junior in high school when my family acquired our first television set. The nation was recovering from the challenges of a major world war. Travel abroad or even a summer vacation near home was a luxury that required a disciplined savings program. Most families were focused on the basics of a comfortable life: a job, a decent home, and food on the table. As our country recovered from the deprivations of the war years, we were optimistic about the future. In my grammar school, my fourth-grade teacher introduced the class to the basics of poetic expression and asked each of us to write our first poem. My poem captured the attitude of most young people during the 1950s: "I live in the land of plenty / I live where men are free / my future has no limit / it all depends on me." This is probably not a sentiment shared by most young people today.

My childhood was spent in a small, smokestack factory town located in a river valley in western New York State. The school system was adequate but far from optimal. My early education was not challenging. I seldom had homework. My mother questioned this anomaly, but my report cards suggested that my schooling was going well. At that time in small-town America, young men were concerned with football, basketball, baseball, and dating someone who impressed their friends. World events were far away and of little concern.

I was the youngest of four children. When it was my turn to attend college, the family finances had been depleted by my elder siblings. I was fortunate to qualify for an athletic scholarship at a small liberal arts college in Pennsylvania. After two years, I applied to transfer to an Ivy League school. Unbeknownst to me, Yale had just completed construction of two new residential colleges and was accepting twice as many transfer students as would normally be the case. It was also fortuitous to have my transcript reviewed by an assistant dean who never missed a wrestling match at Yale. At the time, wrestling was my premier sport. Lady Luck was on my side, and I made the cut.

As a transfer student at Yale, I was ineligible my junior year for intercollegiate athletics. For the first time in my life, I applied my competitive instincts to my academic studies. I was surrounded by students with private school educations and support from wealthy families. This gave me a strong incentive to demonstrate that a kid with a middle-class, public school background could make the grade. I worked hard, and with encouragement and support from some very capable faculty, I morphed from a confirmed jock into an aspiring scholar. To the surprise of everyone, including myself, I graduated with honors.

The Soviet Union had recently launched the first astronaut into orbit, and our nation's leaders were concerned that our country was falling behind in the space race. Congress approved funding for the graduate training of young scientists. The timing was serendipitous. I received a National Science Foundation fellowship for four years of graduate study. My two years at Yale and four years in graduate school completely altered my life. My father had expected me to join him in the building-supply business he managed. Instead I became a university professor. After thirty years of teaching and doing research at Northwestern University, I accepted a position as the managing partner of a small business. This start-up company became a pioneer in the new field that has become known as predictive analytics.

I have provided this personal testimony to demonstrate the value of education. Every young person should have the opportunities and lucky breaks that I enjoyed. How much stronger the American economy would be if all our children had auspicious beginnings. Our nation can do a much better job preparing our children for the future. They cannot vote, but they are the key to our nation's destiny. Spending tax dollars on prescriptions and medical care for seniors limits what can be spent elsewhere. Retirees like me have had a chance to prosper and contribute to society. It is time to give our children the same opportunities that we enjoyed.

What I am proposing in this book has been heavily influenced by other authors. Few ideas are truly new. We benefit from the thoughts of those who have preceded us. Although my proposals are based on a large number of sources, I am especially indebted to the recent writings of a few authors.

My historical references to the early days of our country are based primarily on two books, *American Nations* by Colin Woodard (Penguin Books, 2012) and *The Quartet* by Pulitzer Prize–winning historian Joseph J. Ellis (Alfred A. Knopf, 2015). I strongly recommend both books to any reader who is interested in the political maneuvering that led to the birth of our nation. My references to the historical track record of our Supreme Court are covered in detail in *Injustices* by Ian Millhiser (Nation Books, 2015).

The proposals for altering the three branches of our government (chapter 3) were influenced by retired Supreme Court justice John Paul Stevens in *Six Amendments: How and Why We Should Change the Constitution* (Little, Brown, 2014). My thoughts on our health care system (chapter 5) were heavily influenced by *The Healing of America* by T. R. Reid (Penguin, 2009) and by *Catastrophic Care* by David Goldhill (Alfred A. Knopf, 2013). My suggestions for modernizing our military establishment (chapter 7) were guided by my leisure-time reading of a number of Tom Clancy novels and a recent novel by P. W. Singer and August Cole, *Ghost Fleet* (Houghton Mifflin Harcourt, 2015). Additionally, many of the observations in this chapter are based on technical information from periodicals and internet sources describing recent advances in our country's weapon systems.

The analysis of the economic implications of taxation and government regulations was molded by *Saving Capitalism*, authored by Robert B. Reich (Alfred A. Knopf, 2015); by two books written by Nobel Prize–winning author Joseph E. Stiglitz, *The Price of Inequality* (W. W. Norton, 2012) and *Rewriting the Rules of the American Economy* (W. W. Norton, 2016); and by *A Fine Mess* by T. R. Reid (Penguin, 2017). A major theme that dominates my thinking on the allocation of our nation's resources is that commerce is a powerful antidote for diminishing the human tendency to engage in warfare. This idea is persuasively documented by Steven Pinker in *The Better Angels of Our Nature* (Viking, 2011). The discussion of political tribalism (chapter 10) was motivated by *The Parties Versus the People* (Yale University Press, 2012), written by former congressman Mickey Edwards. What I have written in the concluding chapter was influenced by E. J. Dionne Jr. in *Our Divided Political Heart* (Bloomsbury, 2012).

My colleagues and friends have provided valuable insights and suggestions based on earlier drafts of this manuscript. The final product is more readable and more comprehensive than my initial efforts. I would like to thank Annie Bickley, Ted Bristol, Pam Britton, Linda Carnes, Kevin Kreuz, Ruth Fredericks, Donna Grauer, Parker Maddux, Michael McLain, Werner Neff, Cathy O'Connell, Nick Schmit, Peter Schulkin, David Slate, Carl Ted Stude, Marti Stude, and James Townsend.

Peter W. Frey
February 5, 2019
Cambria, California

INTRODUCTION

Human beings are perhaps never more frightening than when they are convinced beyond doubt that they are right.
—LAURENS VAN DER POST

The recent history of our nation has been deeply disturbing. The optimism of past generations is not shared by young people today. Millions of Americans worry that future generations will be economically less well off than their parents. Why do so many of us no longer believe that tomorrow will be better than yesterday?

Decisions in Washington have damaged our economy and diminished our influence with other nations. In the mid-1990s, Congress removed banking restrictions that had been in place for almost a hundred years. Banks were permitted to combine traditional commercial banking with riskier investing. A frenzy of subprime real estate mortgages in 2005 and 2006 led to the worst economic recession in eighty years, stripping many Americans of their homes and their life savings. To prevent a collapse of our financial system, the government bailed out bankers but failed to provide financial help for average Americans, many of whom lost everything. The economy has subsequently improved, but most of the benefits have accrued to a tiny minority.

Globalization of world trade has reduced job opportunities and heavily impacted our economy. The path of upward mobility has become arduous. Jobs that permit a person to join the middle class are hard to find. For many Americans, the belief in shared prosperity that developed in the aftermath of the Second World War has faded.

In November 2000, five members of the US Supreme Court with a long history of defending states' rights decided that the state of Florida should not conduct a recount of votes in a presidential election in which one candidate appeared to have several hundred more votes than his opponent out of some three million votes cast. The federal court overruled the Florida Supreme Court's decision to reexamine the outcomes in several districts in which numerous irregularities had been observed. In a 5–4 decision, the justices in Washington declared as president the candidate who had won a half million fewer votes nationally than his opponent. The consequences of this decision have been painful.

In September 2001, nineteen religious fanatics, most of whom were from Saudi Arabia, hijacked four commercial airplanes. Two of the planes were flown into the Twin Towers of the World Trade Center in New York City, and two were flown toward Washington, DC, one attacking the Pentagon and the other with the suspected intention of destroying the Capitol. More than twenty-nine hundred Americans died as a result of these terrorist attacks. The United States subsequently attacked Iraq, with a tremendous show of military force. The campaign started with a shock-and-awe assault on Baghdad and followed with a troop invasion. The result was the death of many young soldiers on both sides, the devastation of Iraq's infrastructure, and the eventual expenditure of two trillion dollars of US taxpayers' money. The repercussions of this war have produced a political disaster in the Middle East, with subsequent developments that have destabilized the entire world.

In 1907, Congress passed the Tillman Act, which banned corporate financial contributions to political campaigns. This law was a reaction to the excesses of the Gilded Age (i.e., the 1880s and 1890s) when powerful corporate lobbyists delivered bags of money to influence congressional votes. In 2010, the US Supreme Court overturned the Tillman Act and opened the door once again for corporations to participate financially in politics. Existing legislation that had limited spending by individuals and corporations in political campaigns was declared unconstitutional.

The Supreme Court, in a 5–4 decision, determined that corporations, for legal purposes, have some of the same rights as individuals. The justices reasoned that limitations on corporate campaign spending violated the free speech provision of the First Amendment.

The presidential election in 2016 demonstrated a level of frustration with politics and politicians not seen for many years. A candidate with no experience in government won the Republican nomination. A twenty-six-year legislator from Vermont, a political independent, received millions of votes in the Democratic primaries. Voters supported populist candidates on the theory that new faces and new ideas had to be better than the current options. Political activity in Washington has become a battleground with both major political parties engaged in unproductive disputes. Politicians appear to be more interested in preparing for their next reelection campaign than addressing the long-term interests of the nation.

Sixteen-year Oklahoma congressman Mickey Edwards summarized this perspective in *The Parties Versus the People*: "Too often our elected leaders seem to think of themselves not as trustees for America's future but as members of a political club whose principal obligation is to defeat other Americans who do not share an allegiance to the same club. . . . In today's America, citizens typically are allowed to elect their public leaders from among the narrow menu of choices permitted by our political parties, and from districts drawn to serve party interests; and when these leaders take office—as our putative 'representatives'—it is too often party, not constituent or conscience, that guides their performance."

In his 2013 book, *Coming Apart*, Charles Murray observes, "Washington is in a new Gilded Age of influence peddling that dwarfs anything that has come before" and, "Hundreds of billions of dollars of goodies are now up for grabs for whoever knows the right people, can convince the right committee chairman to insert a clause in the legislation, convince the right regulatory bureaucrat to word a ruling in a certain way, or secure the right appointment to a key government panel." Murray believes that this unseemly behavior is a symptom of a more basic problem of our society. The political and economic elite "have abdicated their responsibility to set and promulgate" traditional standards.

The irony of our current predicament is that there is no shortage of ideas on how to confront these challenges. The problem is a political system that is unequal to the task. Our political leaders are so polarized and so focused on getting reelected that constructive plans and programs supported by a majority of Americans have little chance of being enacted into law. Gridlock in Washington must change. The spirit of political compromise needs to be resurrected from the past.

Every school child learns that our forefathers intended to build "a more perfect union." Jefferson, with his companions' approval, wrote, "We hold these truths to be self-evident, that all men are created equal, that they are endowed by their Creator with certain unalienable Rights, that among these are Life, Liberty and the pursuit of Happiness." Most of us have forgotten that in 1776 this statement of equality and equal rights did not apply to women, men without property, slaves, or Native Americans.

Many years later, Andrew Jackson provided a clearer expression of Jefferson's intentions: "In the full enjoyment of . . . the fruits of superior industry, economy, and virtue, every man is equally entitled to protection by law; but when the laws undertake to add to these natural and just advantages artificial distinctions, to grant titles, gratuities, and excessive privileges, to make the rich richer and the potent more powerful, the humble members of society, the farmers, mechanics, and laborers who have neither the time nor the means of securing like favors to themselves, have a right to complain of the injustice of their Government."[1] Equality means that all of us deserve equal treatment before the law, not that we are carbon copies of each other.

CREATING A LEVEL PLAYING FIELD

Americans enjoy competitive sports. Football, basketball, hockey, and baseball have captured our imagination and provided entertainment for a large segment of the population. The longevity of enthusiasm for these sports derives from competition in which both teams have a fair chance of winning. Competition occurs in an environment in which everyone is subject to the same rules. The playing field tends to be level because both teams have experienced coaches and comparable equipment. We wouldn't think of putting a football player on the field without a helmet and pads and without proper training and preparation.

Our market economy is often quite different. Some players start out with significant advantages. Youngsters from the wealthy suburbs are provided with quality education, proper health care, excellent nutrition, and successful role models. Young people living in the inner city have few of these advantages. The contest is rigged. None other than Abraham Lincoln said, "We do wish to allow the humblest man an equal chance to get rich with everybody else." Each person needs a fair opportunity to compete in our market economy. The world of commerce should have a level playing field.

A level playing field requires equal educational opportunity for all of our children, universal quality health care, and an effective and efficient safety net for youngsters, for the less capable, and for the elderly. A level playing field would provide multiple benefits. Our country would be taking advantage of all of its potential brain power in meeting international competition. Having more financially successful participants in our economy would boost the country's productivity. A larger middle class would mean more consumers and consequently more successful businesses. The American promise of opportunity for all would no longer be a myth.

A level playing field also requires government regulations and taxation that promote competition in the business environment and enable American companies to operate effectively in a global economy.

American corporations should be taxed and regulated in a manner comparable to their international competitors. Health care costs for employees should be covered by our government. We are the only developed nation that expects employers to provide health care for their workers.

Creating a level playing field will be expensive. Providing universal educational opportunity, health care, and a proper safety net will cost trillions of dollars every year. It is wonderful to talk about how to improve our world, but talk is not enough. At election time, politicians propose to improve government services. How to pay for new programs is usually explained with vague general principles or simply ignored. My proposals will address what is needed to improve our economy and what is needed to have a fair political system. I will also suggest a plan for financing these changes.

SUTTON'S LAW

Willie Sutton was born in 1901. He became a habitual bank robber. During his lifetime he stole an estimated $2 million, spent half his adult life in prison, and escaped from prison three times. His use of various disguises earned him the nickname Slick Willie. Asked by a reporter why he robbed banks, Sutton is purported to have answered, "Because that's where the money is."[2] This statement has come to be known as Sutton's Law, a metaphor for focusing problem solving on the most obvious and relevant possibilities.

The largest expenditures in our federal budget are defense spending, health care, and Social Security. Rethinking how we spend government money on these programs with an eye for improvement and reductions in cost would be helpful. Another obvious target for additional income is a taxation system that extracts more from wealthy Americans who have benefited the most from the strong American economy. Enacting modifications for obtaining more income from the financially successful might stimulate the nation's economy and would be a sensible application of Sutton's Law.

Do we have the courage to address the challenges of our modern world? Instead of bemoaning our recent history of unmet challenges, wouldn't it be preferable to make the necessary adjustments and refinements in our political system that can fix the unsolved problems?

The proposals in this book attempt to maintain the governmental objectives of our Founding Fathers in a manner that is compatible with today's technologically advanced economy. Simplistic phrases like "drain the swamp" and "make America great again" resonate well with frustrated voters. Devising effective innovations that actually solve our problems, however, will require more than catchy slogans. A thoughtful plan is needed. This book provides a brief summary of how our nation was formed, discusses the difficulties that have ensued, and offers detailed blueprints for how we can move forward to a more enticing future. The objective is to realign governmental processes to realize our nation's potential by deepening citizen involvement in politics, enhancing economic opportunity, and encouraging individual responsibility.

Chapter 1

————

THE EMERGENCE OF AN AMERICAN NATION

People move forward into the future in the way
they comprehend the past. When we don't understand
something in our past, we are therefore crippled.

— NORMAN MAILER

The history of our country has much to tell us about why our current political and economic situations are so disturbing. In trying to understand who we are and where we are going, it is helpful to examine where we have been. Our current political disagreements are often based on mythology rather than on a realistic knowledge of the past. Discord and dysfunction are not a recent part of our nation's history.

Our country was founded by immigrants who had no desire to replace the restrictions and taxes imposed by a European monarch with similar limitations. The individuals that emigrated from Europe to the United States were fiercely independent, quarrelsome, and contrary. They were not a random sample of the European population. They were younger, healthier, and more courageous than the typical European. Leaving the country where one was born and sailing across a mighty ocean to start a new life is not something that most people attempted. The settlers who came to North America were hearty folk who were traveling into the unknown to escape religious intolerance and to find economic opportunity.

The early settlers represented a diverse set of cultures. The new arrivals in Jamestown and Plymouth had little in common. Some immigrants were wealthy; most were not. Some were extremely religious; some were not. The glue that held the colonists together was a desire for a fresh start. They all wished to escape from intolerable situations in Europe. This combination of cultural diversity and a strong desire for independence produced small enclaves of people who were happy to be geographically separated to do their own thing. Unfortunately, this mixture did not provide an incentive to form a central government that could draw the colonists together to form a nation.

New England was settled by radical Calvinists and other groups who focused on local political control and the creation of homogeneous communities centered on strong religious beliefs.[1] Settled by stable, educated families, New Englanders believed that government could improve individual lives and that tight, well-regulated communities were essential. Aristocratic social arrangements were unwanted. These immigrants were eager to proselytize their beliefs to anyone willing to join them.

The geographic area that is now greater New York City was settled by the Dutch in the seventeenth century. These immigrants were interested in commerce with the intention of founding a global trading society.[2] They were more pragmatic than their New England neighbors, balancing their business interests with their Protestant religious beliefs. They welcomed other ethnic groups who had an interest in trade and introduced their neighbors to the Dutch practices of free speech and tolerance of racial diversity.

English Quakers settled in the area that is now Delaware, southern New Jersey, and southeastern Pennsylvania.[3] These colonists also believed in a pluralistic society. They welcomed others, including

German immigrants, who shared their desire for community independence and freedom from governmental intrusions. Along with their Dutch neighbors, they demonstrated little interest in being involved in a disagreement with the British monarch.

Virginia and its surrounding areas were occupied by the children of English gentry. They came to America because England could not provide the land needed to follow their parents' way of life. Their intention was to re-create a semifeudal manorial society like that in the English countryside. They wished to import the aristocratic traditions they had left behind in England. They envisioned a society in which the political and social affairs were controlled by an elite group of land owners.[4] Initially their land holdings were worked by indentured servants, and somewhat later by slaves. Ideals such as equality of opportunity or public participation in governmental decisions were not part of their heritage.

Immigrants from Ireland, northern England, and Scotland settled in what is now western Virginia and the country beyond through the Cumberland Gap. Many of these people had come to America as indentured servants and had moved farther west after fulfilling their obligations.[5] Many were escaping the strife in the British Isles and seeking an opportunity for a better life. As a group, they prized individual liberty and personal sovereignty and disliked the communal restrictions that typified the fresh arrivals in New England.

Georgia and South Carolina became the new home of slave lords from Barbados in the West Indies. They brought with them white supremacy, aristocratic privilege, and a political system that served to maintain the status quo.[6] Their cruelty and lack of concern for their slaves stood in strong contrast to the egalitarian principles of their northern neighbors. Their descendants maintained a system of racial injustice.

These regional cultures have maintained their identity for several centuries. It seems that the habits and lessons learned in one generation's childhood are passed on to each succeeding generation. The arrival of immigrants from multiple geographic regions often has little impact on these established cultures. The influx of new residents usually reinforces rather than alters the original social and political attitudes. Newly arrived settlers who are troubled by the existing social structure seldom stay.

AN OPPORTUNITY TO BUILD A NATION

Our war for independence from Britain was a temporary partnership against a common threat. The only factor that united the American colonists was their hatred for a distant king who was attempting to control and tax his former subjects. The British Redcoats were unwelcome intruders. The individual cultural regions of the country, however, had no interest in replacing the king of England with an American central government that would reestablish the same restrictions they were fighting to remove.[7]

The Dutch in New York City and their neighbors, the Quakers, had little enthusiasm for fighting the British and acted as neutral third parties during the war. Many colonists seemed ambivalent about engaging in combat.[8] Pro-independence participants demanded loyalty oaths from neighbors suspected of loyalty to the king. In many instances, British sympathizers were ostracized and, on occasion, tarred and feathered. Anglican churches were damaged, and several priests were killed. The battle of King's Mountain was fought between American loyalists and their neighbors who advocated independence. Benjamin Franklin and his son, William, the colonial governor of New Jersey, assisted opposite sides.

Washington took control of the Continental army but had great difficulty obtaining financial support from the individual states. He also found that many state legislatures gave verbal support to his effort but kept their militias at home rather than sending soldiers to fight the British.[9] Most of the American army came from New England and Appalachia. They were a threadbare group often lacking food and military supplies.

In the early years of the hostilities, Washington's forces were easily defeated by the British, the most formidable army and navy in the world. Washington was forced to change his strategy from direct confrontation to a rear-guard, guerrilla-warfare approach. His troops attacked the British only occasionally, and then only at unexpected times and locations. His famous crossing of the Delaware was one of these occasions, routing enemy soldiers who were sleeping in their barracks.

The American victory in the Revolutionary War was not the result of its superior military force. The two major successful battles for the Americans occurred at Saratoga and Yorktown. In the North, the British had planned to consolidate two armies, one led by General Burgoyne in Canada and the other led by General Howe moving from New York City up the Hudson Valley.[10] The plan was to trap an American army near Albany. Burgoyne underestimated the difficulty of moving his military forces south through the heavily timbered Champlain corridor. His trip from Canada became a disaster with the loss of equipment in rugged terrain and the loss of troops to illness and fatigue while trying to cut passage through an impenetrable forest. Distracted by Washington's maneuvering in the New York area, Howe failed to move north to assist his colleague as planned.

At Saratoga, Burgoyne's troops, deserted by their Huron warriors, were surrounded at Bemis Heights in an indefensible position by sixty-five hundred regular troops and fifteen hundred irregulars from the surrounding countryside. The forces were led by General Horatio Gates and General Benedict Arnold, Washington's best infantry commander, along with Colonel Daniel Morgan and his crack regiment of Virginia riflemen. Colonel Thaddeus Kosciusko, a Polish engineer, directed the construction of strong field fortifications on ground overlooking the Hudson River. The American forces prevailed, and British control of the northern region was greatly diminished. This was a turning point in the war. With urging from Benjamin Franklin and Thomas Jefferson, who were in France, King Louis decided to provide additional military aid to the Americans and authorized a powerful French naval fleet to join the conflict.

The British military effort in the South was also ill-fated. General Cornwallis placed his army on the Virginia shore near Yorktown.[11] Washington's army, which had suffered terribly at Valley Forge, spending the winter without proper supplies or shelter, was invigorated when it learned that the French naval fleet had bottled up Cornwallis at Yorktown, preventing him from receiving supplies or departing. Washington's requests for funding and militias from several states fell on deaf ears. He then appealed to Robert Morris, the wealthiest American at the time, for supplies to move his army south to Yorktown. Morris came through, fortunately, using his own credit to secure loans that rescued the Continental army. Washington also received reinforcements from a French military detachment led by Comte de Rochambeau. Washington moved south and laid siege to Cornwallis's army, which was now surrounded on all sides. Without food or access to military reinforcements, Cornwallis surrendered in October 1781.

The British were frustrated with trying to engage an army that avoided direct confrontation. Britain was also involved in a conflict with France in Europe and was eager to recall its military forces from North America. King George determined that Americans were so cantankerous and uncontrollable that attempting to pacify them was not worth the effort. The Treaty of Paris in 1783 ceded all of the land from the Atlantic Ocean to the Mississippi River to the colonists.

The Continental army was disbanded shortly thereafter, without being paid or honored. Washington was filled with despair: "To be disbanded . . . like a set of beggars, needy, distressed, and without prospect . . . will drive every man of Honor and Sensibility to the extreme Horrors of Despair."[12] In the absence of any financial help from state legislatures, Robert Morris once again rose to the occasion and wrote personal checks to pay the soldiers, nearly bankrupting himself.

REPLACING THE ARTICLES OF CONFEDERATION

The Articles of Confederation that the colonists had created to oppose the British king, an arrangement more like today's European Union than a centralized government, had failed to unite the colonists behind the Continental army. Washington and his aide-de-camp, Alexander Hamilton, were convinced that the thirteen states, if they were ever to form a viable nation, needed a different, more centralized form of government.[13] As a result of the Treaty of Paris, Americans had gained a huge landmass, greater in area than England, France, and Spain combined. If the colonists were to take advantage of this opportunity, members of the confederation would need to abandon parochial attitudes and unite to become a nation that could expand westward.

Following the war's end, the representatives to the Confederation Congress were not concerned with building a nation. Instead, they revealed their mutual jealousies and their inability to think beyond the needs of their local communities. The loose organizational structures that had been adopted placed emphasis on local control and protection of provincial interests. James Madison realized that the diversity of political, economic, and religious cultures posed a significant problem for uniting the states into a coherent nation.

Despite the lack of interest in forming a federal government among the state legislatures and their constituents, Madison and John Jay implored Washington to join their effort to revise the loose confederation and create a governmental structure that could address the need for an effective national government. Alexander Hamilton and John Adams were strong allies in initiating this endeavor.

The evidence for making major changes was obvious. The individual states had violated the terms of the Treaty of Paris, stolen land from Native Americans, and failed to cooperate in building roads and canals.[14] Madison was convinced that the confederation was unworkable and destined for eventual collapse. He and Hamilton had little faith in the wisdom of "the people" and advocated a republican form of government in which ordinary citizens would elect local representatives, who in turn, would select individuals for state legislatures. State legislatures, in turn, would choose representatives for the national government. Madison believed this process of filtering would produce an educated and informed national legislature.

Washington was reluctant to become involved in another major undertaking but finally relented and joined the mission. His presence was influential in gaining support for the Constitutional Convention of 1787. The absence of enthusiasm for the project provided an opening for Madison to dictate the agenda to be considered. Once the representatives congregated, they agreed that all issues would be decided by a one-state, one-vote process rather than by proportional representation. This was not what Madison had intended. Throughout the proceedings, the smaller states held a majority of votes over those with much larger populations, namely Virginia, Massachusetts, New York, and Pennsylvania. The distrust among the states and their disinterest in forming a powerful central government produced a convention in which states' rights became a dominant theme.

Two legislative branches were created: the Senate, with equal representation from each state, and the House of Representatives, with proportional representation. The major controversy was the process for selecting a president, the chief executive officer. After much debate, the delegates invented a novel approach, the Electoral College, which was a compromise between one-state, one-vote and proportional representation.

The government conceived in 1787 encompassed unfortunate characteristics that haunt us today. The members of the House were to be elected by popular vote. The two senators from each state and the president were to be elected by delegates selected by the state legislatures. States with large populations—such as New York, Massachusetts, Pennsylvania, and Virginia—had no more voting power in the Senate than states with small populations, such as Rhode Island, Georgia, and Delaware. The House of Representatives was the only legislative unit that involved direct election by the citizens. However, men without property, women, and slaves could not vote. Less than an eighth of the population older than eighteen years of age could cast a ballot. The Constitution also empowered state legislatures to control redistricting for the House of Representatives based on the results of a census to be conducted every tenth year. This provision has led to political gerrymandering today that heavily compromises the principle of one-person, one-vote.

ESTABLISHING THE CONSTITUTION

In 1787, the states south of the Potomac were deeply dependent on slave labor. Despite Jefferson's earlier pronouncement that "all men are created equal," the issue of slavery was the elephant in the room that everyone ignored. Attempting to tackle that issue would have destroyed any hope of forming a new nation.[15]

The participants in Philadelphia agreed that ratification by the individual states would be a take-it-or-leave-it decision. Many of the states offered amendments for consideration, 124 in all, but the major authors treated these as suggestions only and insisted on an up-or-down vote. A compromise that was subsequently added was the Bill of Rights, which addressed many of the objections. Madison, once again, took the lead and created a proposal for the Bill of Rights. The list he selected reflected his own view of what was needed and what should be excluded. He included freedom of religion and freedom of speech to gain the support of the Dutch in New York City. The Second Amendment was added to ensure, with the dissolution of the Continental army, that the individual states could protect their borders. Madison's intent was that those individuals serving in state militias should have the right to bear arms.

The necessity of adopting a new constitution was hotly debated in town hall meetings and in legislatures throughout the states. The votes to accept the Constitution were extremely close, especially in Massachusetts, New York, and Virginia. The vagueness of important procedural details proved to be an advantage for the advocates. The compromises that had been necessary on the issue of states' rights versus federal power were a major disappointment to Washington, Hamilton, and Madison, and they left Philadelphia believing they had failed to accomplish what they had originally intended.

The Constitution created a governmental system that was a compromise between a powerful central government and a collection of loosely controlled, independent states.[16] For the following 220 years, the United States has paid a heavy price for the ambiguities that were left to posterity by the Founding Fathers. The failure to resolve the issue of slavery resulted in a bloody war seventy years later, disrupting commerce, separating families, destroying much of the infrastructure of the Southern states, and leaving scars that remain today. The absence of a clear plan to control westward movement resulted in white migration that decimated 90 percent of the Native Americans. The States' Rights clause in the Bill of Rights, in which those powers not explicitly delegated to the federal government reverted to the states, has been used repeatedly to block progressive efforts to adapt to technological advancements, to protect the less fortunate, and to adjust regulations as the nation's population expanded.

Over the past two centuries, legislation has modified how we are governed. Our governmental structure has evolved gradually with a series of incremental changes. In 1787, the Founding Fathers made no provision for safety nets such as Social Security, Medicare, Medicaid, and food stamps. Issues such as slavery, women's rights, safety standards, child-labor regulations, corporate monopolies, workers' rights, and environmental protection were not addressed. Our nation's population has increased dramatically, and technology has altered how we live.

State and federal legislatures gradually developed programs to deal with urbanization, communication advances, and rapid travel options.

This step-by-step process has produced a plethora of complex, overlapping, and often redundant government programs that address our modern realities in a very inefficient, expensive, and overly bureaucratic manner.

We need to remember Abraham Lincoln's assessment: "The legitimate object of government is to do for a community of people whatever they need to have done, but cannot if at all, or cannot so well for themselves, in their separate and individual capacities."[17] The progressive actions of Theodore Roosevelt were not expressly authorized by our constitution but followed Lincoln's advice. Roosevelt oversaw the enactment of legislation that controlled monopolies, protected workers' rights, and conserved our national environmental treasures. None of these actions could have been anticipated by our Founding Fathers.

Now may be a good time to reexamine the structure of our republic. We should ask if there might be a simpler, more efficient, and less expensive way to govern ourselves. After two hundred years of incremental changes, perhaps it is time to reevaluate and refashion our political system. Our current system encourages legislators to enact laws that emphasize short-term effects. Laws with an impact that will not be observed for several years, such as funding for education or improvements in infrastructure, often have a low priority. There is a tendency to pander to older citizens who have considerable political influence at the voting booth. Social Security and Medicare are well-funded. Programs that directly benefit our children often receive less financial backing. This is an unfruitful way to invest in the future.

The world today is significantly different from the world our Founding Fathers experienced. The constitution that was created in 1787 involved a series of political compromises that reflected the issues that were important at that time. There is no way that individuals living in the late eighteenth century could have anticipated the social, economic, and technological innovations that have subsequently taken place. The goals and aspirations of our Founding Fathers should be valued and respected. Their political accomplishments were remarkable.

They authored a document that provided our country with an auspicious start. It should be our objective to keep faith with their intentions by continuing to build on a great beginning.

We need to examine key aspects of our political system, including health care, education, welfare, taxation, national defense, and the arrangements for electing our governmental representatives. Can we improve the functionality of established practices? In what follows, I review and evaluate proposals from other authors and offer several dozen additional novel prospects. When habitual routines are not producing the outcomes we desire, maybe it is time to seek more effective ways to address life's challenges.

Chapter 2

INTERPRETING
THE LAW

*You must clear your mind of the fancy . . . that the institutions under
which we live . . . are natural, like the weather. They are not. . . .
We take it for granted that they have always existed and must
always exist. . . . That is a dangerous mistake.*

— GEORGE BERNARD SHAW

The Founding Fathers created three branches of government. They were aware that the Constitution and the laws set by the legislatures would be open to interpretation. Not everyone would view the law through the same pair of lenses. It takes only two lawyers to reach two or more different perspectives. To address this issue, the Founders established a Supreme Court with the power to settle disputes that might arise. Supreme Court justices were to be appointed by the president with the consent of a majority of senators. Congress was empowered to set the number of justices. In 1801, the number was set at five, then at seven in 1807, nine in 1837, and ten in 1863. In 1866, the number was reset to seven, and then finally to nine by the Judiciary Act in 1869. The decisions of the Supreme Court were to be final and immune to reversal by the other two branches of the union. The only remedy for judicial tyranny is a constitutional amendment or, in some cases, new legislation.

This arrangement is actually somewhat peculiar. Political theorists favor a balance of power among the three branches of government. The president can veto legislation passed by majority votes in both chambers of the legislature. However, this veto is not absolute. It can be overturned by a two-thirds vote in both the Senate and the House. In 1787, no provision was entertained to provide oversight of Supreme Court decisions. Neither the president nor the legislatures had any option for changing a Supreme Court decision. Since 1869, five of the nine unelected judges in black robes have been able to make decisions with dictatorial power.

From today's perspective, many of the past decisions reached by the Supreme Court are disquieting. The ruling in 1857 that black people were not citizens in *Dred Scott v. Sandford* was an unfortunate prelude to the Civil War.[1] The Court considered the original intent of the men who had created our constitution and concluded that "it is impossible to believe that" the rights enjoyed by white citizens "were intended to be extended" to people of African descent. Furthermore, the Court stated that black people "had no rights that the white man was bound to respect."

In 1876, in *United States v. Cruikshank*, the Court interpreted the Fourteenth Amendment in a manner that seems to be inconsistent with its wording. Section 1 of the amendment reads, "No State shall make or enforce any law which shall abridge the privileges or immunities of citizens of the United States; nor shall any State deprive any person of life, liberty, or property, without due process of law; nor deny to any person within its jurisdiction the equal protection of the laws."[2] Cruikshank, with several white followers, trapped a group of freedmen in a local courthouse and executed all of them. The Supreme Court, citing the Tenth Amendment (regarding states' rights), decreed that enforcement of the Fourteenth Amendment should be left to the states. This decision and the Jim Crow legislation in Southern states that followed fostered a reign of white-on-black terrorism for many decades.

The Court continued to interpret the Fourteenth Amendment to limit the rights of former slaves. In *Plessy v. Ferguson* in 1896, the Supreme Court justices decided that segregated railway cars were consistent with the Constitution: "The enforced separation of the races . . . neither abridges the privileges or immunities of the colored man, nor deprives him of his property without due process of law, nor denies him equal protection of the laws."[3] Chief Justice Field also supported the practice of excluding African Americans from juries and commented that giving black people the right to serve on juries would require giving the same right to women.

The Court, in its opinion on the Chinese Exclusion Act of 1882, extended racial bigotry to individuals of Asian origin.[4] Chinese laborers were prohibited from entering the United States for ten years. In 1888, the Court also determined that it was constitutional to prohibit Chinese workers who departed from the United States from returning.[5]

Article I of the Constitution gave the federal government the power to "regulate commerce . . . among the several states." In the *Sugar Trust Case* in 1895, and in other cases, the Court employed a highly restrictive definition of the word *commerce*: "Manufacturing, agriculture, mining and production" were not commerce and therefore could not be regulated by the federal government.[6] This ruling essentially gave large corporate interests (such as mining, logging, and rail service) free rein to operate as they pleased. Legislation in several states that restricted child labor, limited working hours, and established safety standards were declared unconstitutional. The Court argued, "The general right to make a contract in relation to business is part of the liberty of the individual protected by the Fourteenth Amendment."

In the last two decades of the nineteenth century, the railroad barons amassed great fortunes by building monopolies and creating trusts that permitted companies to conspire to control prices and the availability of services. The Court ruled that these practices were legal but that the workers' rights to organize for better working conditions and better pay were not.[7] Collusion among corporations was not forbidden by the Constitution but collusion among workers was illegal. Workers had the right to bargain individually with employers but not to bargain collectively.

Efforts by state legislatures to end these practices were repeatedly blocked by the Supreme Court. When railroad workers organized a massive strike for better pay and improved working conditions at the dawn of the twentieth century, the federal government, with approval of the Court, appointed deputy marshals—selected and paid by the railroads—to suppress the strike.

The Court, in the late nineteenth century, also determined that income from capital—ownership of land, stock, or commodities—could not be taxed. The Court had no problem, however, with a tax on wages. Robber barons such as Cornelius Vanderbilt, Leland Stanford, George Pullman, and John D. Rockefeller amassed great fortunes while their workers suffered from low wages and hostile working conditions. At the start of the twentieth century, working conditions were abysmal. In 1916, Congress approved the Keating-Owen Child Labor Act prohibiting the shipping of goods produced by child labor.[8] The Court declared this ban on child labor to be unconstitutional. Previous Court actions had upheld bans on lotteries and prostitution but protecting the health and safety of children and limiting the working hours per day were determined to be an overreach by the federal government.

One of the Court's most egregious decisions was *Buck v. Bell* in 1924.[9] Carrie Buck was born in poverty and indentured for child care to an uncaring family. She was unable to attend school and worked long hours each day. A lower court determined that she was feebleminded. Despite the absence of relevant evidence, the Supreme Court upheld a decision to sterilize her, even though the Constitution provides no basis for such action.

At the height of the Great Depression, President Roosevelt attempted to revive the economy by creating government programs to provide jobs for unemployed Americans. FDR also advocated the creation of a safety net for older Americans. The Court, citing constitutional restrictions on legislative power, determined that the federal government lacked the authority to make these changes.[10] Programs such as Social Security, the income tax, and the right for workers to organize were enacted only after one of the five conservative justices defected to the progressive side of the Court.

When war broke out with Japan and Germany in the 1940s, a hundred thousand Americans of Japanese descent were ordered to leave their homes and were sent to internment camps in rural areas. In *Korematsu v. United States* in 1944, the Supreme Court condoned this deplorable violation of the Constitution.[11] At that time, Americans feared a Japanese invasion and believed that residents of Japanese descent might aid the enemy. However, the evidence that Japanese Americans posed a threat to the country's security was minimal. Many young Japanese men served and died for our country fighting against Germany in Europe.

It is difficult to understand why the reason for sending American citizens of Japanese ancestry to concentration camps was not also applied to American citizens of German ancestry. The Court's decision would appear to be based more on racial bias than on judicial logic.

In modern times, the Supreme Court has also made consequential decisions of a highly controversial nature. The decision to determine the winner in the 2000 presidential election, by overruling the actions of the Florida Supreme Court, was a novel assertion of authority that had no legal precedent.[12] The Court's justification for its action, based on "equal weight accorded to each vote and the equal dignity owed each voter," had no precedent and has subsequently not had any influence on the Court's decisions. Notably, the Court has not been concerned that this principle directly conflicts with the constitutional provisions for the Electoral College and the composition of the Senate.

In 2010, the Court, in the *Citizens United* case, determined that the legislature's effort to restrict massive financial contributions to political campaigns by wealthy people and corporations was unconstitutional.[13]

This decision overturned legislation (i.e., the Tillman Act) that had been established law for a century. The justification was based on freedom of speech and on the proposition that the Bill of Rights applies to corporations as well as individual citizens. The Court also ruled in 2014 that individuals and corporations had the right to contribute to political campaigns without disclosing their identities. For many ordinary citizens, these two findings implied that the Court was providing legal authority for wealthy Americans and powerful corporations to buy elections.

Corporate lobbyists currently have the opportunity to meet with a legislator and offer a proposal for a special consideration that is fine-tuned to benefit the lobbyist's company. This suggestion is accompanied by an offer to provide funding for the legislator's upcoming reelection campaign. This is hardly different from old-fashioned bribery in which a bag of cash was offered. What is even more pernicious is the lobbyist's opportunity, thanks to the financial largesse of the company he or she represents, to suggest that his or her company might make a $5 million contribution to the legislator's opponent in the upcoming election if the legislator opposes the proposal. This amounts essentially to political blackmail. *Citizens United* provides both a powerful carrot and a devastating stick that forces our representatives in Washington to choose between what is helpful for reelection and what is best for the nation.

In his historical review of Supreme Court decisions over the past two hundred years, Ian Millhiser observes, "There appear to be more Americans who believe in wizards and witches than those who believe that unlimited election spending does not lead to corruption."[14] It just so happens that five of these rare individuals sat on the Supreme Court (SCOTUS). Between 2008, the last presidential election before *Citizens United*, and 2012, the first presidential election after the SCOTUS decision, spending by non-campaign groups rose by 245 percent in the presidential election, 662 percent in House races, and 1,338 percent in Senate races.

The decisions of the men who framed our constitution were based on their experience with the world in which they lived. Our modern world is incredibly different from the society experienced by our Founding Fathers. Our legal system has been constructed in an incremental fashion, with each new law engineered to be consistent with the Constitution and prior legislation. This process has produced requirements and restrictions that were appropriate during the early years of our country but may not be suitable for our society today.

The issues in question have often had little resemblance to bygone circumstances. Sensible legislation has been annulled for lack of a precedent in prior legal rulings. Adjudicating legal cases in a manner that is consistent with past court cases is often counterproductive when the issues in question bear very little resemblance to bygone circumstances. Many of these decisions have limited citizens' freedom and have overruled legislative actions designed to address the nation's problems.

THE SECOND AMENDMENT

The Bill of Rights was adopted in 1791. Because the Continental army had been disbanded, the individual states sought a guarantee that the federal government would not restrict their authority to defend their territories from intruders. The Second Amendment addressed this concern: "A well-regulated Militia, being necessary to the security of a free State, the right of the people to keep and bear Arms, shall not be infringed." At that time, the Second Amendment was not intended to address the right of private individuals to own guns for hunting or for Americans to own guns to defend their homes against criminals. In frontier America, those rights were uncontested. The amendment's focus was on the state governments' obligation to have the military capability to defend their citizens from foreign intrusions or other actions that might threaten public order.

Retired Supreme Court justice John Paul Stevens has suggested that the Founding Fathers would have made their intentions somewhat clearer if the text of the Second Amendment had read, "A well-regulated Militia, being necessary to the security of a free State, the right of the people to keep and bear Arms *when serving in the Militia* shall not be infringed."[15] It is also germane to note that the original wording specifies "a well-regulated Militia." This is inconsistent with the interpretation that every citizen should be free to own and operate deadly weapons.

The framers of the Constitution would have also anticipated that the phrase "to keep and bear Arms" referred to an individual owning a musket or a handgun. In 1791, a rifle was a single-shot device that was loaded by placing powder and a projectile directly into the barrel of the gun. These muzzle loaders, when operated by an experienced soldier, required approximately thirty seconds before a second round could be fired. This type of weapon was much less lethal than today's rapid-fire equipment. Modern technology has created realities that our ancestors could not have anticipated.

For almost two hundred years, the courts held that the universal right to bear arms applied to military service only and that individual states could place limitations on gun ownership by private citizens. It has only been in the past three decades that the courts have constrained state and federal legal power to limit citizens' gun rights. In 5–4 decisions, the Supreme Court determined that commonsense curbs on gun ownership are unconstitutional. Because of these court decisions, state legislatures are prevented from passing laws in regard to who can own a gun, what types of guns are appropriate for private ownership, and whether individuals can be restricted from carrying guns in certain locations. The Court's decisions have made it difficult to keep firearms out of the hands of known criminals, people with mental health issues, and individuals on the federal government's no-fly list.

In 1971 in an interview on PBS, Chief Justice Warren Burger, a conservative Republican appointed by President Richard Nixon, observed, "If I were writing the Bill of Rights now, there wouldn't be any such thing as the Second Amendment. This has been the subject of the greatest fraud on the American people by special interest groups in my lifetime."[16]

It is unfortunate that the Supreme Court restricts individual states from enforcing commonsense gun regulations. Military-style weapons are not necessary for hunting or home defense, and yet convicted felons and individuals with serious mental disabilities are permitted to openly carry these lethal weapons. A ban on military-style assault weapons was in effect from 1994 to 2004. During that time, there were eighty-nine deaths caused by assault weapons. Between 2004 and 2014, when assault weapons were once again available to the public, they were the cause of more than three hundred deaths.[17] Interpreting the Second Amendment in a way that protects an individual's right to own a military-style weapon (such as the AR-15) would seem to be logically consistent with granting individuals the right to own any type of modern weaponry, including a .55-caliber machine gun or a shoulder-mounted missile launcher.

In the United States, gun violence kills people over twenty times more often than in other wealthy countries.[18] Americans own almost as many guns as all of the other civilians in the rest of the world.[19] Rather than placing restrictions on gun ownership, our federal government prohibits states and municipalities from legislating restraints. Given the instability of the human psyche, is it sensible to permit civilians to own deadly weapons that are not needed for hunting or home defense?

However, gun ownership may not be the key issue. Switzerland has the third-highest ratio of civilian firearm ownership in the world. The Swiss thoughtfully regulate who can own a gun and how guns are stored. Owners are required to acquire proficiency in handling firearms. Gun homicides in Switzerland are ten times less frequent than in the United States.[20]

Americans *should* have the right to own a firearm. Since guns can be used to kill people, however, the right to operate a gun should be regulated in the same way that we currently regulate the privilege of driving a car. A license should be required. The licensing process should be similar to what is required to qualify for a driver's license. Each applicant should pass a written test and a field test that demonstrates his or her competence to handle a weapon properly. Applicants convicted of a crime or having a drug or alcohol addiction should not receive a license. Concealed-carry permits should be limited to police officers or registered security agents.

The type of weapon available to nonmilitary personnel should also be regulated. Weapons used for hunting, sporting contests, or home defense should be legal. On the other hand, civilians should not have access to military-style rifles. Equipment available to private citizens should be capable of firing no more than six times without reloading. The firing mechanism should also restrict the discharge rate to three seconds or more. These sensible mechanical limitations would prevent firearm-initiated public massacres without compromising a gun owner's ability to hunt or to defend his or her home.

———

In 1821, Jefferson looked back at what had been accomplished in 1787. His observations provide a thoughtful consideration of the role our constitution should play: "Some men look at constitutions with sanctimonious reverence, and deem them, like the ark of the covenant, too sacred to be touched. They ascribe to the preceding age a wisdom more than human and suppose what they did to be beyond amendment. I knew the age well; I belonged to it and labored with it. It deserved well of its country. . . . But I know also, that laws and institutions must go hand in hand with the progress of the human mind. As that becomes more developed, more enlightened, as new discoveries are made, new truths discovered . . . institutions must advance also, and keep pace with the times. We might as well require a man to wear still the coat which fitted him as a boy as civilized society to remain ever under the regime of their barbarous ancestors."[21]

Albert Beveridge was the keynote speaker at the 1912 Progressive Party convention that nominated Theodore Roosevelt. He echoed Jefferson's assessment: "The constitution is a living thing, growing with the people's growth, strengthening with the people's strength, aiding the people in their struggle for life, liberty, and the pursuit of happiness, permitting the people to meet all their needs as conditions change."[22]

Maybe it is time that the iron-handed judicial process put in place by the Founding Fathers should be altered. Making decisions with a backward-looking legal system may not always be an optimal process for dealing with the complexities of our rapidly changing world. In recent years, there have been cases in which past precedents provide no relevant guidelines. Our heavily constrained legal process may produce an unwise decision. Court judgments on gun control, gerrymandering, and political financing would appear to be seriously at variance with basic common sense. Should five of the nine justices have unconstrained power to overrule the president, the Senate, and the House of Representatives?

The Founders' intention for a governmental system with checks and balances was not implemented with respect to the Supreme Court. We might consider establishing parity among the three branches of government. A simple and reasonable amendment to the Constitution would provide legislative oversight of the Supreme Court. The House and Senate can overrule presidential vetoes with a two-thirds vote in both chambers. Why not amend our constitution to provide a similar provision for legislative action that could overturn decisions by the Supreme Court?

Chapter 3

ONE CITIZEN, ONE VOTE

Loyalty to a petrified opinion never
yet broke a chain or freed a human soul.
— MARK TWAIN

O ur contemporary understanding of democracy is a political system in which the people directly elect the individuals who determine how a country functions. A basic premise of democracy is that each citizen has an equal say in the election of governmental officials: one person, one vote. Although Americans routinely boast about our democracy, our system of government is actually a republic.

The president is elected by the Electoral College not by the will of the majority. The election of two senators from each state also grossly violates the principle of one-person, one-vote. Wyoming with 586,000 citizens has the same number of senators as California with 39.2 million citizens. Each voter in Wyoming has sixty-seven times as much voting power in selecting senators as a voter in California. The forty-six Democratic senators in the 114th Congress received a total of 67.8 million votes. The fifty-four Republican senators received 47.1 million votes.

The allocation of seats in the United States Senate does not appear to follow any rational plan. Maine, New Hampshire, and Vermont, three contiguous states, have a combined population of 3,291,000 and a combined land area of 49,083 square miles. California has 39,200,000 citizens and a land area of 155,973 square miles. The three states have six senators while California has two. Montana, North Dakota, South Dakota, and Wyoming, four contiguous states, have a combined population of 3,251,000 and a land area of 387,553 square miles. Texas has 27,863,000 citizens and a land area of 261,914 square miles. The four states have eight senators, and Texas has two. It would be sensible to have the land areas that currently make up Maine, New Hampshire, and Vermont combined into a single state. It would also be reasonable to combine the land areas of Montana, North Dakota, South Dakota, and Wyoming into a single state. These two alterations would provide more balance in how our citizens are represented in Washington.

Puerto Rico, an American possession, has more American citizens than twenty of our states, but has zero senators, zero representatives in the House, and no votes in the Electoral College. The District of Columbia has 681,000 citizens and occupies 68 square miles of land. Alaska has 742,000 citizens and covers a territory of 570,374 square miles. Both entities have three electoral votes. It is difficult to find a rationale that considers population and land area to determine how federal political influence is allocated.

Population density also seems to be irrelevant to representation. New Jersey with two senators has 1,206 persons per square mile. Wyoming, also with two senators, has 6 persons per square mile, and Alaska with two senators has 1 person per square mile. Whose idea was this?

The election of individuals to the House of Representatives is based, in theory, on proportional representation. Our forefathers decided that the House districts would be redefined every ten years after the census had been taken. This was needed because the country's population was growing unevenly across the various states. Our forefathers also decided that this process of redistricting would be done by the individual state legislatures. This was a serious mistake. Essentially, politicians were given a license to select the voters who would populate each federal House district. This has led to a serious problem: gerrymandering. Over time, the politicians in each state have become adept at designing new voting districts in a way that creates major advantages for the political party in control of the state legislature.

The government created in the late eighteenth century was a remarkable achievement. However, it was not a tablet of stone carried down from the mountain after a long conversation with the Supreme Being. Our forefathers faced a difficult challenge: to create a governmental system that could be adopted by states with diverse cultures and competing priorities. The Founders accomplished a near miracle by gaining agreement among constituents who simply wanted to be left alone and who were suspicious of the motives of their peers.

It is reasonable to conclude, from a perspective gained 225 years after our Founding Fathers created a nation, that the job they did was less than perfect. Monday-morning quarterbacking profits from twenty-twenty hindsight. It is time for us to make revisions in our government's structure that honor our forefathers' intentions with adjustments that meet the realities of our modern world.

ELECTING THE PRESIDENT

The procedure for electing our president could be simplified and made more democratic. The president is the only federal official that represents all Americans. He or she should be elected by popular vote. Every registered voter in every state should have one vote. The Electoral College disenfranchises a significant number of voters in a majority of the states. More than thirty states have a history of domination by one of the two political parties. Residents in the minority party in each of these states have no power to influence the outcome of the presidential election. With two exceptions—Maine and Nebraska—all of the Electoral votes go to the winner of the state whether the margin is 51–49 or 95–5.

The Electoral College was a novel political construction that Madison believed was necessary to gain support for the proposed constitution from the Southern states. A large proportion of the population in the South consisted of slaves. In determining the composition of the House of Representatives and the number of electors from each state in the presidential election, a compromise was reached in which each slave was counted as a three-fifth addition to the population count. This increased Southern representation in the House and also increased the number of votes in the Electoral College for the states with slaves. It is not a strange outcome that eight of the first nine presidents came from Virginia. Without the thirteen extra electoral votes created by Southern slavery, John Adams would have won the presidential election in 1800.

Alexander Hamilton also provided another justification for the Electoral College. The electors were intended to be "men capable of analyzing the qualities adapted to the station, and acting under circumstances favorable to deliberation, and to a judicious combination of all the reasons and inducements which were proper to govern their choice."[1] If the person chosen by the will of the people, as expressed in the popular vote, were antithetical to constitutional values, the electors were empowered to select an alternative. In modern times, this option has not been invoked. Electors have essentially rubber-stamped the outcome at the polling booths. The intended protection provided by the Electoral College against the election of a populist demagogue has not been effective. Given the political rationale for the Electoral College based on slavery and the absence of its use as intended by Hamilton, there seems to be no sensible reason why this practice should remain in force today.

In 1967, the American Bar Association described the continued use of the Electoral College as "archaic, undemocratic . . . and dangerous."[2] This assessment has had no impact on how we are governed probably because constitutional amendments are very arduous undertakings, requiring a two-thirds vote in both houses of Congress and ratification by three-quarters of the states. There is no rational justification for our country continuing to elect presidents with this dated methodology.

In the presidential election in November 2000, Albert Gore received 544,000 more votes than George W. Bush. After five justices of the US Supreme Court ruled that Florida could not recount votes in a flawed election, Bush became president on the basis of an Electoral College majority. In the 2016 presidential election, Hillary Clinton received 2,871,000 more votes than her opponent. Donald Trump, however, became president because he had more Electoral College votes. American history might be dramatically different if our presidents had been elected by popular vote.

If the Electoral College were abolished, every voter, no matter the location of his or her residence, would have equal influence on the election. The officials would count every vote that was cast across all of the states, and the candidate with the most votes would be declared the winner. What could be simpler? What could be more democratic? Why has our country retained a voting procedure for the election of the president that is very complicated, difficult to justify, and antidemocratic?

ELECTION OF SENATORS

The Constitution also provides for two senators from each state. In 1790, the non-slave populations of Virginia (455,000), Pennsylvania (431,000), Massachusetts (379,000), and New York (319,000) were much larger than the non-slave populations of Rhode Island (68,000), Delaware (58,000), and Georgia (53,000).[3] The number of citizens per Senate vote in the four large states averaged 198,000. The same measure in the three small states was 29,800. The citizens in the small states had more than six times the voting power for electing senators. This relationship is not consistent with one-person, one-vote.

The United States now has fifty states rather than thirteen, and our population has grown to approximately 320 million residents. The inequality in voting power for representation in the Senate has also grown. Today the four states with the largest populations are California (39.2 million), Texas (26.4 million), New York (19.6 million), and Florida (19.6 million). The four states with the smallest populations are Wyoming (0.58 million), Vermont (0.63 million), North Dakota (0.72 million), and Alaska (0.74 million).[4] The 104 million citizens in the four large-population states have eight senators. The 2.7 million citizens in the four small-population states also have eight senators. Today, the citizens in these four rural states have thirty-nine times more voting power in electing senators than the residents in the four urban states. Both the election of the president, given our Electoral College, and the election of senators separate the power of a state's votes from the number of people casting ballots.

Our Founding Fathers could not have imagined our nation today, with 320 million residents, spanning the entire continent from the Atlantic coast to the Pacific Ocean. Revising the makeup of the Senate by making representation proportional to the populations in each state would depart markedly from the objective of those who met in Philadelphia in 1787. Is there a compromise that might reduce the large variation in the voting power of citizens in different states?

A revision that might be sensible, without seriously departing from the Founders' intentions, would be to have three senators in the ten largest-population states, one senator in each of the ten smallest-population states, and two senators in the remaining states. The identity of these states would be determined once each decade when the census was taken. This would retain the current size of the Senate (one hundred senators) and would also retain a voting arrangement in which the smaller-population states have more influence than would be the case with proportional representation. This change would reduce, however, the substantial unanticipated increase in voting power that has occurred over many decades for residents in states with very small populations.

The ten largest-population states today are, in order, California,

Texas, New York, Florida, Illinois, Pennsylvania, Ohio, Georgia, Michigan, and North Carolina. The ten smallest-population states are Wyoming, Vermont, North Dakota, Alaska, South Dakota, Delaware, Montana, Rhode Island, New Hampshire, and Maine. Among the ten largest-population states, there are three blue states, three red states, and four purple states. Among the ten smallest-population states, five are red states, four are blue states, and one is a purple state. The proposed realignment of the seats in the Senate would not have a large impact on the balance of power among the two major political parties.

ELECTING MEMBERS OF THE HOUSE

The composition of the House of Representatives in 1787 was intended to provide proportional representation. The arrangement that was created for redistricting, however, has become a serious problem not anticipated by the Founding Fathers. Control of redistricting by state politicians has led to the creation of districts that seriously compromise the fairness of the voting process. Partisan redistricting efforts are very effective given the capabilities of modern computers and the availability of detailed databases. District lines can be chosen by observing party registration numbers and prior election results from each precinct (and sometimes even smaller geographic units). With sophisticated software and elaborate maps, politicians can create districts in which the likely outcome of an election is known in advance. In most states this process takes place behind closed doors with no public oversight. The result is that politicians choose the voters rather than having the voters elect the politicians.

In all but thirteen states, the political party in control of the state legislature creates districts in which the voters favoring the opposition party are "packed" into a small number of districts. For example, several districts might be created in which 90 percent of the voters are individuals who voted for the candidate of the opposition party in the previous elections. The rest of the districts are constructed to provide a clear majority (e.g., 60–40) favoring the party in control. This strategy produces more districts for those in charge than one would expect based on the relative number of supporters for the two political parties.

The effect of this corrupting effort can be seen in nine purple states in the 2012 election.[5] In the House of Representatives elections in these nine states, the Democratic candidates received a total of 20,098,682 votes (50.6 percent) while the Republican candidates received a total of 19,647,175 votes (49.4 percent). This approximate fifty-fifty split of the votes would suggest that the two parties' representation in the House from these nine states would be essentially fifty-fifty. Figure 3.1 illustrates that this was not the case.

State	Democrat Votes	Republican Votes	Democrat Seats	Republican Seats
Florida	4,265,854	4,055,920	10	17
Indiana	1,125,893	1,378,644	2	7
Michigan	2,556,997	2,075,515	5	9
Missouri	1,188,050	1,492,472	2	6
North Carolina	2,164,761	2,249,392	4	9
Ohio	2,693,139	2,513,244	4	12
Pennsylvania	2,852,948	2,603,232	5	13
Virginia	1,806,025	1,876,761	3	8
Wisconsin	1,445,015	1,401,995	3	5
Total	20,098,682	19,647,175	38	86

Figure 3.1: Gerrymandered Representation in the House in 2012

Surprise! The Republicans controlled the state legislatures in these nine states and used their redistricting prerogative to pack Democratic voters into a small number of districts. The actual representation in Congress for these nine states was thirty-eight Democrats and eighty-six Republicans. Even though the Democratic voters were in the majority, the winners sent to Washington were predominately Republican. If the representation from these states reflected the balance in the votes cast, the Republican party would have had 210 representatives in Congress, and the Democratic party would have had 225. Without these gerrymandered districts, the Democrats would have controlled the House of Representatives. Overall, Democratic House candidates in the 2012 general election received four hundred thousand more votes than the Republican candidates for the House. The Founding Fathers established the House of Representatives to reflect the popular vote, essentially one-person, one-vote. Partisan gerrymandering has invalidated that intention.

In the early days of our nation, there were no dominant political parties as we have today. There also were no computers to fine-tune district borders to give one of the parties a major advantage. It is reasonable to believe that the Founders would not have assigned the responsibility for redistricting to state politicians if they had been aware of the consequence. The capability of modern computers to create partisan districts has produced district maps that defy even the most imaginative expectations.

An example is Congressional District 30 (figure 3.2), created in 1991 by the Texas state legislature. The lack of compactness and the district's complex profile suggests that the Texas authors were not making use of existing city, county, and geographical boundaries. It is difficult to find a rationale for the shape of this district unless one considers partisan advantage.

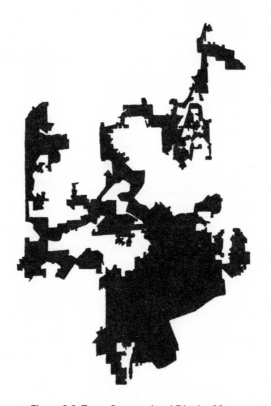

Figure 3.2: Texas Congressional District 30

Retired Supreme Court justice John Paul Stevens wrote in his book *Six Amendments*, "The public interest, rather than mere partisan advantage, should provide the basic standard that should govern the design of electoral districts. . . . There is no reason why partisans should be permitted to draw lines that have no justification other than enhancing their power. . . . The gerrymandering process makes elections . . . less competitive, and leads candidates, whether liberal or conservative, to adopt more extreme positions."[6] Ending political gerrymandering will help promote political compromise. In the 2004 decision on *Vieth v. Jubelirer*, Stevens explained his dissent to the Court decision: "If no neutral criterion can be identified to justify the lines drawn, and if the only possible explanation for a district's bizarre shape is a naked desire to increase partisan strength, then such a district is a violation of a state's duty to govern impartially and an impermissible political gerrymander."

Because voters have been carefully sorted into districts where the nonpartisan voter has no influence, elections are controlled by the most extreme activists in both parties. Primary voters, who tend to be the most polarized, determine who will represent each congressional district. Representatives in gerrymandered "safe districts" are only vulnerable to a candidate in their party's primary election who may be more extreme. The person selected in the primary need not worry about serious competition from the representative of the other party. For this reason, the House of Representatives is unable to govern a diverse society in which rational discussion and compromise are required to pass legislation. Middle-of-the-road voters have been disenfranchised by political gerrymandering and have lost control of the political process. The failure of the House of Representatives in recent years to accomplish even its basic responsibilities, such as preparing and passing a federal budget, is a direct consequence of the polarization induced by gerrymandering.

It is not surprising that voter turnout in gerrymandered districts tends to decline. Voters quickly learn that their votes will not influence who wins. Why bother to vote when the outcome of the election is predetermined? Our democracy is diminished when elections are not competitive. Incumbents become unresponsive to their constituents because only the party activists have votes that count. Representatives become more extreme and less willing to compromise.

IMPARTIAL REDISTRICTING

Our system of government would be greatly improved if redistricting were handled by a committee of nonpoliticians dedicated to fairness in representation. This is difficult since well-meaning participants can disagree regarding what is and is not fair. Also, because of the political importance of the district maps, the committee members are likely to be offered generous bribes to vote in a way that favors the donors.

Another approach would be to establish guidelines for how districts can be redrawn by state legislators. In November 2010, Florida voters passed two amendments to the state constitution that limited politicians' options for gerrymandering districts. The two amendments outlawed districts that would deny meaningful participation by minorities; required districts to be contiguous, compact, and equal in population; and when feasible, required districts to make use of existing city and county boundaries, and geographical features, such as rivers. Even with these guidelines, politicians in Florida have created district maps that still reflect serious gerrymandering. Residents in urban areas tend to vote for Democratic candidates while rural and suburban voters are more likely to prefer Republicans. Requiring districts to be compact often results in lopsided partisan districts.

A better solution for opponents of gerrymandering would be to redistrict using a computer to create districts that were consistent with several nonpartisan objectives. The data that are available at the precinct level and, in some cases, at the block level, include the results of previous elections, racial and age breakdowns for each area, information from internet activity, and many other details of interest to mapmakers.

A computer can be programmed to build districts that optimize several goals. For example, the computer could be instructed to seek equal populations and a minimal total perimeter for each district. It could also have guidelines to make use of existing city, county, and geographical boundaries. In addition, the districts could avoid extreme partisan imbalance in respect to party voting in the most recent presidential election. This effort to achieve partisan symmetry in each district would force redistricting to more closely follow the one-person, one-vote principle. This would produce compact districts that are highly competitive. Wouldn't it make sense to have House districts that conform to sensible, voter-determined guidelines instead of ones created by representatives with technical staff assistance to maximize partisan advantage?

Newly formed districts should be required to meet several objectives. For example, no district in the state would be allowed to have a ratio between the circumference of the perimeter and its area that was greater than a predetermined value. This would ensure reasonably compact districts. The procedure could also require that all districts would be approximately equal in population based on census data. Differences would have to be within one or two percentiles. A third criterion would limit the maximum permitted discrepancy in party registration in each district. The difference between the number of registered Republicans and registered Democrats would not be allowed to exceed a set value, such as a 10 percent difference. Creating districts that jointly satisfied these criteria would be difficult for mere mortals. For a modern computer, however, this operation would be a routine optimization problem.

With partisan symmetry, there would be several hundred competitive House districts instead of thirty as is currently the case. With a small number of competitive districts, wealthy individuals and corporations with campaign money can shape election outcomes. If there were several hundred competitive districts, contributors would need massive financial resources to influence all of the elections. Participation would require targeted expenditures, and this should diminish the role of big money in federal elections.

Competitive districts would greatly increase voter turnout because every vote would influence who would win. In recent elections, many eligible voters have not participated. This is especially true of young Americans. In the 2012 election, only 38 percent of voters younger than twenty-five cast a ballot. In contrast, 70 percent of seniors, those citizens older than sixty-five, cast ballots.[7] If every voter were important in determining who would win, we might observe much higher rates of involvement.

Another advantage of competitive districts would be pressure on incumbents to be responsive to their constituents. Also, the need for term-limit legislation would be reduced since an incumbent who was not representing the interests of his or her district or the country as a whole would be less likely to be reelected.

A fourth advantage would be a strong incentive for representatives to take more moderate positions on legislation. In safe districts, incumbents, to retain their seats, have to fight primary battles against candidates that are more extreme on issues. Many representatives, in both parties, are more worried about being replaced by an opponent in their own party than by the opponent in the general election. Incumbents with moderate views, those individuals in the middle of the road, have been frequently run over.

Currently, there are some hopeful signs that this serious quandary may finally be getting some attention. Legislators in North Carolina, Pennsylvania, Wisconsin, and Ohio are seeking judicial actions that would require their states to develop a redistricting process that more closely approximates the goal of one-person, one-vote.

UNIFORM VOTING PROCEDURES

The Founding Fathers did not specify a uniform set of requirements for voting in federal elections. Over the past two centuries, states have developed criteria for voting that favor the political party that controls the state legislature. The party in power determines voter registration requirements and the location and operational hours of polling stations. Voter suppression has become a common tool.[8] Between 2011 and 2015, almost four hundred voting restrictions were implemented among the various states.

Some states have created registration requirements that discourage targeted demographic groups.[9] Restricting the voting rights of persons convicted of a felony eliminates many potential voters. States in which there has been racial prejudice in dispensing justice are especially likely to disenfranchise former felons. Accepting only a driver's license or a passport for registration unfairly limits eligibility. Some states accept a hunting license but not a college ID. Some states do not permit same-day registration even when the vote is not counted until the person's eligibility has been validated. Individuals working two jobs often have difficulty acquiring the necessary registration documents prior to the election.

Another common tactic by officials managing elections is the reduction of voting locations in areas heavily populated by supporters of the other party.[10] Voters must travel long distances and often have to wait in long lines to cast their ballots. This is a serious disincentive for many potential voters. Providing an opportunity to vote by mail is an appropriate antidote for this chicanery. Many states do not provide this option.

Several states remove potential voters from the registration rolls if they have not voted in recent elections. This often eliminates citizens who otherwise would be completely qualified to vote. Additional partisan deviousness has been observed in some voting locations. Individuals in the registration office only remove recently inactive voters previously registered with the "wrong" party.

Our nation needs to set uniform standards for voting eligibility in federal elections. Universal standards applying to all fifty states should specify who is qualified to vote, what the requirements for registering should be, what procedures are legitimate for collecting votes, and what technical requirements need to be in place for voting equipment. Permitting each state to set its own rules and standards has produced fifty different voting systems that have been manipulated for partisan advantage. Why not modify our voting procedures and alter our government institutions to provide a level political playing field for all our citizens? Would it not be appropriate to supplant the current disparate voting systems with a common set of rules?

Chapter 4

———

A UNIVERSAL
SAFETY NET

*In the final analysis, our most common basic link is that we all
inhabit the same small planet. We all breathe the same air.
We all cherish our children's future. And we are all mortal.*
— JOHN F. KENNEDY

The first requirement for a level playing field is a simple guarantee
that each person, especially a child or young adult, has food to eat
and a place to sleep at night. We don't send athletes onto the field who
are malnourished or unable to find shelter. Is it reasonable to expect
a hungry, homeless person to participate successfully in our nation's
economy? Should access to life, liberty, and the pursuit of happiness be
available only to those born to wealthy parents?

History has proven that a market economy has been much
more effective in producing vital goods and services than alternative
arrangements. Bottom-up consumerism has been more successful than
top-down government control. Despite the clear superiority of a free
market approach, there are individuals in America who have not fared
well. In our modern society, the very young, the very old, people with
physical or mental handicaps, and those with insufficient education or
job training are often left behind.

During the Great Depression, President Roosevelt introduced Social Security to help older Americans who were unable to cope with the failed economy. Subsequently, over many decades, our government has added new programs to assist individuals who would otherwise have difficulty acquiring food and shelter. These include welfare for single women with children, Section 8 (housing subsidies), Supplemental Nutrition Assistance Program (food stamps), Medicaid, National School Lunch Program, School Breakfast Program, Earned Income Tax Credit, Temporary Assistance to Needy Families, Supplemental Security Income, and other social-service arrangements. Developed in an incremental fashion, they entail complex bureaucratic systems for administration. These well-intentioned programs often overlap, providing opportunities for people to game the system. Supplemental income often ends when a person becomes gainfully employed, discouraging recipients from seeking low-wage jobs. Another problem with current social-service policies is that recipients are often stigmatized for depending on government handouts.

Our welfare system, constructed over many years by diverse government officials, is neither efficient nor cost-effective. The recipients are often unhappy, the administrators are backed up with heavy workloads, and taxpayers wonder why the cost is so high. It may be time to think about cleaning house. Why not make an assessment of what is needed to help those who have been left behind and replace the current patchwork arrangements with an uncomplicated, unified system?

In Switzerland, Finland, and in several cities in the Netherlands, legislators have proposed a universal monthly stipend. The Green Party in Britain in the 2015 election advocated a Citizen's Basic Income program. The idea is to be certain that every person has an income that covers life's essential needs, whether or not the person is gainfully employed. Swiss government officials were concerned that this approach would be too expensive and would encourage workers to quit their jobs.[1] Unlike my proposal, the Swiss stipend was to be an addition to the current welfare programs rather than a replacement for them. The proposition was offered to the voters in a referendum. It was defeated by a lopsided majority. It is not clear whether this negative decision was a rejection of the central idea or whether the Swiss electorate believed that combining a universal stipend with existing welfare programs was financially impractical.

Surprisingly, history tells us that this proposal is not novel. In fact, it dates back to the Enlightenment, being suggested and endorsed by such notables as the Marquis de Condorcet and Thomas Paine. In 1979, the conservative economist F. A. Hayek added his endorsement to this idea. This approach has also been actively discussed by contemporary economists and others, including Milton Friedman, Anthony Atkinson, Paul Krugman, Charles Murray,[2] and Robert B. Reich.[3]

The cost of a universal safety net (USN) depends on several factors: the amount of the stipend, who is eligible, and whether the stipend replaces or adds to the current welfare system. How large the monthly stipend should be depends on the purpose of the stipend. If the idea is to grant a comfortable living for every recipient, the plan would be far too expensive. On the other hand, if the objective is to offer sufficient income for each person to purchase food and have a roof over his or her head, the cost is not an insurmountable problem. A universal stipend that provides a safety net is a reasonable goal.

Eligibility for the stipend would depend on age and length of citizenship. When a young person reaches age eighteen, he or she would become eligible if—and only if—he or she has been a US citizen for at least two years. Specifying a length of citizenship for qualification is essential since the program should not be a magnet for immigrants who wish to avoid the necessity of finding employment. Monitoring age and citizenship is not complicated. This would reduce the number of fraudulent payments.

The stipend should be sufficient to cover basic needs but not enough to discourage the recipient from looking for a job. In today's world, a monthly stipend of $800 for each citizen would be reasonable. Each recipient would specify a local bank that offers debit cards. The stipend would be electronically transmitted to the recipient's debit account. This would avoid the need for a complex bureaucracy to administer payments.

To cover the cost of these stipends, the USN system would be a substitute for (rather than an addition to) the current federal welfare system. The transition to this novel arrangement would be challenging but feasible. Social Security and other programs, such as food stamps and Temporary Assistance for Needy Families, would be eliminated. A major portion of the cost of the new safety net would be covered by transfers from existing welfare programs.

In addition to the assets that are currently distributed to needy recipients, the USN program would gain funding by reducing management expenses. These include the expense of determining who is currently eligible for subsidies and the amounts each person should receive. Having a single program with a simple eligibility requirement is more efficient and increases the percentage of expenditures that actually go to recipients.

Implementation of these changes would most likely require a period of time when both the new and old systems would operate side-by-side. Young people could opt to transfer to the USN system while older people could remain on Social Security. This would increase government expenditures during the transition period.

The monthly stipend proposed for the USN system would be inadequate for seniors when they retired. The monthly amount that I have proposed ($800) would be a poor replacement for Social Security. To address this deficiency, the government should require all employees, along with their employers, to each remit 2.5 percent of each paycheck into a personal retirement account. These accounts would provide a defined-contribution retirement program for every citizen. The payments would be invested in the employee's name and would travel with the person when he or she changed jobs. The contributions to this account would start with the very first paycheck and would continue with each new job until the person retired.

The funds in these retirement accounts would be invested in qualified stock, bond, and real estate vehicles in a conservative, balanced portfolio. Unlike Social Security, each person's account would grow steadily over time. The individual's retirement money would not be compromised by a corporate bankruptcy nor by a legislative adjustment necessitated by lack of public funding. This plan would also apply to employment arrangements that do not currently provide fringe benefits. Anyone who receives a paycheck would be enrolled in the program.

At age sixty-five or anytime thereafter, the owner of the account could begin withdrawals of the money in monthly payments gauged to last for the person's expected lifetime. These monthly withdrawals, combined with continued universal safety net stipends plus personal savings, should provide a comfortable retirement. Social Security depends on funding from current tax income. The trillions of dollars that have been contributed to Social Security over the past several decades have already been spent by our government. This would not be the case with defined-contribution personal accounts.

These deductions from the employee's paycheck and additions to the employer's costs would be small in comparison to the current requirements for both Social Security and Medicare, which total 6.2 percent for workers and another 6.2 percent for employers. Since my health care proposal eliminates payroll deductions for Medicare (see chapter 5), both workers and employers would enjoy a reduction of 3.7 percent in mandatory contributions to the federal government. Self-employed individuals, who now contribute 12.4 percent of their income for Social Security and Medicare, would contribute 5 percent to their retirement accounts.

Would a guaranteed monthly stipend discourage employment? There is concern that providing a "free ride" for every adult citizen would reduce the number of people interested in working for a living.

This might be true for some people. Although there are limited empirical data on this issue, the information that is available is encouraging. In the 1970s, Manitoba, a Canadian province, experimented with a guaranteed income program.[4] The overall participation in the labor market remained fairly steady. Later analysis indicated that less money was spent in the province on mental-health services and hospital visits. Having a stable income appears to be good for mental and physical health. A recent survey in Switzerland asked citizens whether a universal basic income would cause them to stop working. Only 2 percent of the respondents answered affirmatively.

A population survey on individuals between twenty-five and fifty-four conducted in 2015 indicated that 18 percent of unmarried males and 23 percent of unmarried females were currently unemployed. Many of these young people were living at home with their parents. The universal stipend would augment funds available for advanced education and job training. The USN, along with universal health care (see chapter 5) and supplemental funds for tuition (see chapter 6), might help more young people prepare to join the workforce.

Individuals with a base income might also be more likely to accept a wage level that would otherwise be unacceptable without the stipend. This would permit more people, including older people with low skill levels, to join our country's workforce. Getting one's "foot in the door" is a powerful stepping stone to advance to an improved wage or a better job. It is likely that a USN would augment the number of wage earners who contribute to our economy.

Two-person households would also benefit greatly from a USN program. Couples with children could have one full-time job and one part-time job, allowing the parents to spend more time with family. Children who start life with improved parental support are more likely to become successful adults. Our economy would benefit. The stipend might also reduce crime. Additional entry-level jobs for young people and more parents at home might deter unlawful activity.

In addition, adults with a stable income would have less incentive for illegal activity.

There are many other advantages of a universal safety net. The current welfare system, based on top-down government controls, is a highly inefficient method for income redistribution. A bureaucratic workforce commonly produces rules that fail to consider important individual differences among the recipients. It is difficult to tailor services to the needs of diverse local communities and special cases. Putting the money, without strings attached, into the bank accounts of individuals maximizes expenditures that meet the real needs of the recipients. A consumer-oriented system is more productive than one controlled by bureaucrats.

A USN would also eliminate a major problem of many current welfare systems. When a recipient gains employment and begins to earn income, the welfare benefit is often discontinued or gradually reduced. This reduction in the monetary value of the job decreases the person's incentive to continue working. With a USN, every dollar the person earns adds to his or her income. Getting a job does not decrease the stipend.

There are also several psychological advantages of a USN program. Everyone likes to believe that he or she is a contributing member of society. Being on welfare within our current system can blemish a recipient's sense of self-worth. With a USN, every adult receives a stipend; there is no stigma attached to the monthly deposit that appears in his or her debit account. The current welfare system heavily influences self-esteem, physical health, and, ultimately, mortality.

Having a universal safety net might also discourage individuals from blaming the system for their own personal failures. With a stable source of income to cover food and shelter, there are fewer excuses for not getting one's act together. In the absence of psychological problems, there would no longer be a reason for being homeless or for begging on street corners. By providing additional income to low-income families, a USN might also decrease the number of blighted urban areas.

Another advantage of a USN is its potential impact on federal minimum wage regulations. Trying to determine what the appropriate level should be for a mandated minimum wage is difficult. Different parts of our nation have very different economic environments. What is needed for a decent living in New York City or San Francisco is not the same as what would be needed in rural America. Trying to set a uniform wage requirement for the whole country may not be the best way to approach this issue.

With every citizen receiving a monthly stipend from the federal government, our country would not need to have a federal minimum wage. Employers would be able to offer pay scales based on local conditions. Young people would be able to gain experience while receiving a relatively low starting salary or hourly rate. The newly hired people who perform well would be valuable to their employers and would be in a strong position to seek a raise. The employer would be much more likely to hire new workers knowing that he or she could evaluate employees in terms of their productivity and pay them accordingly.

One might think that providing a stipend to wealthy citizens would be a terrible waste of taxpayers' money. However, the money saved by eliminating the bureaucracy for determining who should qualify and for adjudicating cases when someone demands inclusion would be substantial. In addition, all recipients would be subject to taxation rates that reflect the impact of the universal stipend. A significant portion of what would be received by wealthy individuals would come back to the government in personal income taxes. If a wealthy person were offended by accepting such a stipend, he or she could return the funds to the federal treasury.

Most economists believe that distributing additional money to needy people is a significant stimulant to the nation's economy. Evidence suggests that individuals at the low end of the income distribution tend to spend almost all of their income at the time it is received. For wealthy people this number is approximately 70 percent of their income. The universal safety net should increase consumer spending.

With more customers, American businesses would be more profitable. There would be more jobs and our government would collect more income taxes.

A basic income program, supported by private donations, will be launched in 2019 with a pilot group of about a hundred people in Stockton, California by twenty-seven-year-old mayor Michael Tubbs. The program provides a $500 monthly check for low-income residents and a $1,000 college scholarship for public high school graduates. This first-in-the-nation project will be closely watched by advocates and skeptics.[5]

———————

Trickle-up economics would have a more powerful positive impact on our economy than trickle-down economics. Wouldn't increasing the number of consumers be a more effective way to energize commerce than providing targeted advantages to the one percent? From a moral perspective, justice in a market economy requires that every citizen receive, at minimum, a small financial subsidy to join the competition. Might a universal stipend also be the most sensible way to address the employment dislocations produced by technological advancements?

Chapter 5

MARKET-BASED UNIVERSAL HEALTH CARE

Ever since I was a little girl I poured all the medicine doctors ever gave me down the drain and planted their pills in my flower pots.
—EDMONA COLLINS, ON HER 99TH BIRTHDAY

The second ingredient for a level playing field is universal health care. In a market economy, it is only fair that each person participates without the handicap of a curable illness or an injury that can be repaired. Is it reasonable to expect individuals with serious health problems to compete successfully? The US Army's recruiting mantra is on target: "Be all you can be."

From the perspective of other developed nations, our health care system is less than optimal. Medical expenditures in the United States in recent years have averaged 18 percent of gross domestic product (GDP). The comparable numbers for other first-world nations are 11 percent in Sweden, 11 percent in France, 11 percent in Germany, 10 percent in Canada, 10 percent in Britain, 9 percent in Australia, and 7 percent in South Korea.[1] Unlike in the United States, all these countries provide single-payer government health care systems. Everyone is covered. The quality of care in these other countries equals or exceeds our system on a number of international measuring surveys. Health statistics indicate that other developed nations have longer life expectancies, better recovery rates, and lower infant mortality.[2] The United States also has hundreds of thousands of citizens each year that go bankrupt because of an inability to pay for medical services. This does not happen in comparable nations.

With the exception of Britain and Canada, these countries have no waiting lines.[3] Even in Britain and Canada acute care is provided without any delay. Patients elsewhere also have free choice among doctors and hospitals, and insurance companies cannot exclude patients for preexisting conditions or avoid payment based on a technicality. Japan stands out with a cradle-to-grave system that residents treasure; annual expenditures total $3,000 per person as compared to $7,000 per person in the United States.[4]

Universal health care in these other countries combines public and private providers. Some nations incorporate private, not-for-profit insurance companies that compete for customers while others involve national health insurance programs. Most of these countries provide services with doctors and nurses as independent contractors. The medical arrangements that would appear to be examples of "socialized medicine" exist in Cuba and, surprisingly, in the United States. The US Department of Veteran Affairs and the Indian Health Service for Native Americans are two of the few systems that provide health care with government-owned hospitals and government-employed doctors and nurses.[5]

The United States spends billions of dollars to protect our citizens from terrorism. This investment might save, on average, a few hundred lives each year. The absence of universal health care in the United States leads to premature deaths of more than twenty thousand Americans each year from medical problems that could be successfully treated.[6] The major reason is that these unfortunate people cannot afford to go to a doctor or hospital. For wealthy people and those with high-end insurance, the United States provides medical services that compare favorably with all other countries on the planet. The United States also leads the world in research and in the development of new treatments and new pharmaceuticals. However, our medical care is expensive, of uneven quality, and often involves poor customer service. Why not improve this system?

High cost is not a mystery.[7] Our providers—doctors, nurses, hospitals, and pharmaceutical companies—are paid more than in other developed countries. In other nations, doctors, hospital administrators, and pharmaceutical company managers seldom drive luxury cars or belong to exclusive country clubs. The cost of hospital stays and treatments with medical equipment, such as MRI and CT scans, are also significantly greater in the US. Administrative expenses are exorbitant. Between 1975 and 2010, the number of doctors rose by 150 percent. The number of health care administrators expanded by 3,200 percent. Delivering a baby in America costs, on average, more than $10,000. In Britain, France, Spain, and New Zealand, the cost is less than $4,000.

When Americans go to a pharmacy to fill a prescription, they routinely pay two to three times as much as patients elsewhere. We are the only country in the world that permits advertising of prescription drugs. In many instances, this policy encourages patients to request medications that are unnecessary and sometimes harmful. For fear of losing patients, doctors often will prescribe a requested drug if they don't anticipate negative side effects. These unneeded medicines add to the cost of medical care since these additions to the patient's bill have to be covered by higher insurance rates.

In Europe and Japan, medical students and nurses receive substantial public educational support. Young people do not acquire massive debt obligations along with their medical degrees. This removes some of the negative aspects of lower salaries once they are employed. This arrangement also means that a wider range of candidates are able to enter the profession.

Our health care system is the only one among developed countries that is financed by insurance companies that make a profit for their shareholders. Without shareholders, foreign insurance companies pay for medical expenditures and pay wages to their employees but have no shareholders expecting dividend income. Americans spend approximately 25 to 30 percent for administrative overhead as compared to 15 percent in these other industrialized countries. Bringing these costs in line with Europe and Japan would reduce our country's $3 trillion medical expenditures by $450 billion. For-profit insurance companies add substantially to the price of medical services due to marketing expenses and dividends to shareholders. This is an unnecessary expense.[8]

In Spain, the widespread use of community health centers reduces cost and provides efficient care of common, uncomplicated medical problems. Primary care, medical advice, and routine medical services are provided within local neighborhoods. Often these services are available in the evenings and on weekends. By avoiding expensive trips to hospital emergency rooms, patients receive necessary care at a dramatically lower expense.

Instead of having hundreds of incompatible and overlapping administrative procedures, other nations have developed uniform methods of describing, recording, and pricing services.[9] The United States is the only developed nation in which health care expenditures vary dramatically from one locale to another. For example, spending on Medicare varies from approximately $4,000 per enrollee in Nevada to almost $11,000 in North Dakota.

Several countries, including France and Germany, employ a universal smart card for each patient, which keeps a record of all medical services, including diagnoses, treatments, hospital stays, pharmaceutical prescriptions, outcomes, and billing information.[10] These electronic systems simplify record keeping and billing and greatly reduce administrative expenses and clerical errors. Since every person carries a smart card at all times, emergency doctors can access the patient's information when there is an unexpected medical crisis.

In most countries, government-sponsored health care does not exclude citizens' options for private medical care. Private and public systems often coexist side-by-side. Wealthy individuals are free to buy high-end medical services if they so wish. Surprisingly, this option is not exercised very frequently.

In 2016, health care expenses in America were $10,348 per person.[11] According to the Kaiser Foundation, this is approximately twice as much as the average expended in countries of comparable wealth. Comparison of our health care with others suggests that quality care and universal coverage can be achieved for much less than we are currently spending. The United States has been a leader in providing a wide range of goods and services for its citizens at reasonable prices. Why not apply the same approach to health care? A major advantage of a market economy is its ability to use bottom-up pressure from consumers to influence price and quality.

To improve health care in the United States, we need to have patients who are also consumers.[12] Currently, bills are paid by insurance companies, not patients. Seniors on Medicare and younger patients with insurance coverage seldom know the cost of the procedures they receive. When a doctor recommends a diagnostic test or proposes a treatment or writes a prescription, neither the doctor nor the patient is commonly aware of the financial repercussions. How often do patients ask questions about prices?

A recent AARP–University of Michigan study discovered that most patients (60 percent) believe that doctors are unaware of the price of the prescriptions they write. Doctors also seldom (28 percent) discuss drug costs with patients.[13] Neither doctors (34 percent) nor pharmacists (22 percent) tend to recommend a lower-priced prescription drug when one is available. It is foreordained that medical services and prescriptions will be expensive when the decision makers are not paying attention to the costs of the various alternatives. When patients become consumers, the health care industry will begin to allocate resources properly, improve efficiency, and innovate.

MEDICAL INSURANCE

The American insurance model for covering medical services is also a strange arrangement. The purpose of an insurance contract is to spread the expense of a low-probability event (like a tornado, flood, or forest fire) among a large group of people who each face that risk. The overall cost for each individual is affordable because the event that is being insured occurs only rarely. Insurance for health care does not fit this model.[14] Medical insurance contracts are very expensive because the events being insured occur frequently. Our health risks are not easily spread across a large group of individuals. Health problems are not low-probability events. They are inevitable, even for very healthy people, because all of us face the physical disabilities of our senior years.

Because most Americans depend on insurance programs to cover medical expenses, very few consider alternatives that might be better. If medical patients were weighing the relative costs of various alternatives, they might be making different decisions. Exercise, nutrition, public safety, and emotional balance are more important in determining how healthy we are than how often we visit a doctor or go to a hospital. The most common causes of early death are heart disease, cancer, diabetes, homicide, suicide, and auto accidents. The first three of these causes are influenced much more by what we eat, how we exercise, and our lifestyle choices than by professional health services.

If we had to directly confront physician bills and hospital bills, we might consider paying more attention to exercise and nutrition. Preventing health problems by altering our behavioral decisions would save money and also make us healthier and happier. Health experts routinely remind us of these realities. The Centers for Disease Control and

Prevention remind us that lack of physical activity, poor nutrition, and tobacco use are responsible for much of the illness, suffering, and early death related to chronic diseases.[15]

We are told that today's seniors are the healthiest generation in history. If so, why are we always going to see a doctor? Citizens on Medicare spend much more time with physicians than did their parents and grandparents. They take more diagnostic tests and consume more prescription drugs than prior generations. Medical professionals benefit financially from all this additional activity, but the American taxpayer ends up covering the bill. Many of these services may be unneeded and, in some cases, may actually be dangerous.[16]

Medicare is in financial trouble. People who became eligible for Medicare in 2013 paid, on average, $60,000 into the program. Estimates indicate that each person will use $170,000 in benefits.[17] Since current contributions by employees to Medicare are spent immediately rather than invested, a college degree in mathematics is not needed to realize that this system is unsustainable.

The issue is not whether we should change our health care system, but when and how. We have the advantage of observing what other countries have done to provide care. We can examine their efforts and determine what does and does not work. Other countries provide universal health care that costs a great deal less than our complex arrangements, and by accepted medical standards, provide a level of quality that is at least as good as what we experience here in the United States.

Our country is a leader in medical research and in developing groundbreaking new treatment options. Technological advances in other parts of our economy have greatly reduced the price of goods and services. In contrast, new medical equipment and new pharmaceuticals have increased costs. Without price discipline and without competition for customers, the medical industry has no incentive to consider cost in recommending diagnostic tests or treatment alternatives. There is a better way to provide medical care.

Singapore provides quality universal health care at a cost considerably below other developed countries.[18] With a population of 5.2 million and an average income comparable to the United States ($50,000), Singapore employs an unusual approach. All employees are required to contribute a percentage of their earnings to a health service account. These funds can be used to cover family medical expenses and to pay premiums on a catastrophic insurance plan.

The government maintains an insurance program to cover severe disabilities and a fund to pay medical bills for the financially indigent. Individuals have the option to purchase additional private health insurance without any subsidy from the government. The government covers everyone for approximately 4 percent of GDP. This is by far the least expensive plan that provides universal health care. The coverage is limited within reasonable bounds. This provides a strong financial incentive for patients to consider the cost of various medical options and to shop for the best quality at the most attractive price.

THE GOLDHILL PLAN

David Goldhill, in his book *Catastrophic Care*, has proposed a modified form of the Singapore system for the United States. He recommends a bottom-up approach in which patients act as consumers, purchasing medical services in the same manner they would acquire other services. He summarizes this perspective: "Prices are signals that drive the allocation of resources, encourage innovation and competition, and force efficiency. Because we don't acknowledge their existence in health care, prices have a hard time doing their job."[19]

Goldhill's proposal is meant as a replacement for Medicare, Medicaid, and the Affordable Care Act (i.e., Obamacare). There are three major components in his plan. Every person has a health service account. The government deposits $8,500 each year on the person's birthday starting when he or she is born. This amount is slightly less than the average yearly amount spent in the United States on health care for each individual today. These funds are restricted to expenditures on health care. Over a number of years, each person's health service account (HSA) would accumulate a significant balance because most young people do not require extensive medical care.

Every person is required to purchase catastrophic health insurance for major medical expenses. This insurance covers only truly catastrophic illnesses or injuries. Any illness or accident that costs less than, say, $40,000, would not be considered catastrophic. When insurance is used only for rare, truly major unpredictable health disasters, it becomes affordable.

Since it would be used infrequently and be spread across a large number of individuals, this insurance could be maintained with yearly premiums of approximately $1,500. This would be especially feasible if the health insurance companies were private, nonprofit entities as is the case in most of the world. This annual insurance deduction would leave approximately $7,000 as the yearly increment to each person's health service account.

For a young person with a major illness costing less than the catastrophic insurance threshold, the plan would permit him or her to borrow against future deposits in the account. It would also be feasible to permit family members or friends with significant balances in their HSAs to help cover the expenses. If a person's HSA has a balance when the person dies, the remaining funds would be transferred from his or her estate, tax-free, to one or more other HSAs.

The bureaucratic disaster that now exists in our health care system could be replaced with a smart card (like those used in France and Germany) that not only records each person's life history of health information but also acts as a debit card to transfer money from the HSA to make payments. A computerized system would authorize expenditures from the HSA to prevent fraudulent transactions that were unrelated to medical services. A federal agency would determine which providers were qualified to receive payments and which medical treatments qualified for payment. With a unified system based on modern technology, payments could be made within a few days of service, and analytical software could detect fraudulent transactions. Current payment systems—such as Medicare, Medicaid, and Obamacare—have serious problems with medical fraud. Reducing fraud would save hundreds of millions, if not billions, of dollars.

Since most of the government contributions to the health service accounts would remain unused for many years, the immediate financial impact on government resources would be less than what one might expect. If current trends remain, most of the withdrawals from these accounts would occur after people reach age sixty. Older Americans consume the lion's share of medical expenditures. While the government's financial obligation would be guaranteed, most responsible young people would try to avoid unnecessary expenditures in order to be better prepared for the needs of their senior years. During the early years, a person's HSA could accumulate more than $250,000.

The Goldhill plan would provide universal health coverage for everyone and would introduce a powerful incentive for cost control. Introducing consumerism into health care would be a dramatic revision for this behemoth industry. As customers, patients would seek the safest, highest-quality service at the best price. Reviews that are now common with restaurant and hotel experiences, as well as with many other service industries, could become the norm in health care. Consumers sharing information would have a powerful effect on the entire industry. Market forces are long overdue in the health care arena. Imagine a health care system in which providers would have to compete for customers. A bottom-up market system would provide cost control in health care in the same way that it does in all other aspects of the American economy.

It is reasonable to expect that a health care system based on service accounts and nonprofit catastrophic health insurance accounts could reduce America's medical costs from 18 percent of GDP to something like 12 percent of GDP. This price is in the same range as other nations' universal programs that provide excellent care with no waiting lines. Considering Singapore's experience, a system based on service accounts might actually provide quality medical care for less than 12 percent of GDP.

The initial transition to this type of system does not have to be a huge financial shock to our federal budget. Since the system would be a replacement for Medicare, Medicaid, Obamacare, and the Children's Health Insurance Program, a major portion of the funding would be transfers from these programs. Older people would be grandfathered under the current system. Initial funding of the health service accounts for young people would be primarily paper transfers since most would have limited health expenses. Their accounts would grow, but the funds would remain largely unspent until their senior years, when their medical needs would increase. Creating market forces that restrain outlandish spending on health care is long overdue.

END-OF-LIFE CARE

Another consideration that is difficult to discuss and even harder to address is end-of-life care.[20] In the past 120 years, global life span, from birth to death, has increased on average by approximately 40 years. In developed countries today, an adult male at age fifty can expect to live thirteen more years than did his predecessors in 1900. A serious complication of improved medical technology is the prospect of living one's final years in a nearly vegetative state. In many cases, elderly patients have difficulty recognizing members of their own family. Other terminal patients spend months confined in bed with full-time nurses required for even the most basic life-preserving necessities.

In the past, seniors often died at home surrounded by family. Today, especially in wealthy countries, they are more likely to die in a hospital or a senior-care unit. It is very common for death to be preceded by a surge of expensive treatments that are essentially pointless. Many of these seniors would be happier to avoid the pain and the indignities of modern end-of-life care. When the illness is clearly terminal, the patient should be given a choice of options. Being rolled over in bed as if one were a piece of meat or conversing with family and caretakers with the intellectual capabilities of a child are not ways most of us would like to be remembered.

A recent survey in four developed nations found that a majority of people would prefer to die at home rather than in a hospital.[21] A majority of people would also prefer to die without pain, discomfort, and stress. The reality is that many seniors experience confusion, depression, and pain during their final years. There is an enormous difference between what people say they would prefer and what they are likely to receive. Surprisingly, patients treated with palliative care live as long as others receiving customary medical procedures. This humane approach should be employed more frequently.

The high cost of traditional end-of-life care can be a serious burden for families. Many seniors would prefer to have their hard-earned lifetime savings go to their children and grandchildren rather than to pay for medical treatments that have no benefit for anyone. Seniors should have a choice to end their lives without pain or fanfare when they no longer believe that life is worth living.

Reshaping our health care services to exist within a market-based system should improve the quality of care and significantly reduce costs. Medical care is a business and like any other business, competition for customers will produce better outcomes for patients. A system that works well in Singapore is very likely to be effective in our country also. Our current system is unsustainable. Wouldn't it be a good idea to investigate an alternative that has worked well elsewhere?

Chapter 6

EDUCATIONAL OPPORTUNITY

The school is the last expenditure upon which
America should be willing to economize.
— FRANKLIN D. ROOSEVELT

The composition of the American workforce has evolved over the past five decades. In the 1960s, high school graduates were just as likely to be employed as college graduates. Today those who have finished college have a distinct advantage. Employment opportunities for workers without present-day skills have diminished. Wages have also mirrored this change. In the 1960s, less-educated men earned 80 percent as much as college graduates. By 2014, that proportion had become 60 percent.[1]

As technological advancements disrupt employment opportunities, our high schools, colleges, and universities need to prepare our young people for new employment options. Brain power and knowledge acquisition will be the keys to success. Increasing our investment in education at all levels is necessary if our country is to remain competitive in the global economy. The United States should also augment traditional options with an inexpensive trade school pathway that combines on-the-job training with specialized classwork. This would permit prospective mechanics, electricians, plumbers, and carpenters to acquire the sophisticated skills that will be needed for a successful career in our increasingly technical world.

NOVEL EMPLOYMENT OPPORTUNITIES

Two centuries ago, in Britain, the invention of machines that could do work previously requiring human labor began the industrial revolution. Workers feared that machines would deprive them of gainful employment. People dependent on manual labor for their livelihoods were threatened by new inventions. What had been a stable source of employment was slipping from their grasp.

Automation displaces people who do routine, repetitive tasks. This is true for both manual labor and white-collar office work. Technological innovations have broadened the applications that can be targeted. Taxi and delivery drivers, receptionists, security guards, cashiers, telemarketers, and accountants are all vulnerable. Some jobs requiring fine motor skills, sensory awareness of the environment, and thoughtful decision making are being done more efficiently by machines than by humans. In our modern, high-tech world, a highly trained but specialized worker, such as a radiologist, can be replaced by a computer.

Silicon brains are efficient, tireless, and increasingly less expensive. Computer chips don't ask for wage increases, longer vacations, or additional fringe benefits. Employers need not face expenditures for employees' benefits. Automating the workplace offers major cost reductions and could cause millions of people to lose their jobs.

With economic opportunities scarce for the majority, a small number of very wealthy people could gain control of our society. The science fiction novels depicting gated communities guarded by military robots for the 1 percent and impoverished shanty towns for the 99 percent might become the norm. The people who own and control the machines could become a domineering plutocracy.

This frightening scenario, however, is one possible outcome of these innovations, but it's not the likeliest. Workers survived and prospered after the disruptions of the industrial revolution. Technology not only eliminates existing professions but also creates opportunities that never existed before. Previous predictions of joblessness have been mostly wrong. History indicates that technological advancement usually generates more work than it destroys. Jobs are not so much lost as they are redefined. Joel Mokyr, an economic historian at Northwestern University, observes that "we can't predict what jobs will be created in the future, but it's always been like that."[2]

The invention of the automobile produced a major decline in horse-related jobs. However, this improvement in human mobility has had a widespread impact on all aspects of our economy. New employment opportunities were devised. Workers were needed to build, market, and repair cars. Someone had to pave modern roads and construct bridges. Trucks and taxis required drivers. Attendants were needed for gas stations. Driver education became a new profession. Increased mobility expanded employment opportunities. It is difficult to imagine today's robust economy in the absence of automobiles. The creation of intelligent machines will have the same impact on our society as did the development of modern transportation options. There will be new jobs, but these employment opportunities will require advanced skills.

INVESTING IN OUR WORKFORCE

As technological innovations alter the workplace, the skills needed to competently operate new equipment also evolve. Humans, however, resist change and are often slow to learn new skills. In the future, employment will require the ability to embrace novelty and to acquire unfamiliar technical expertise swiftly. To be successful in a globalized economy, countries need to maximize the productive capacity of every citizen. Many nations fail to educate women. Ignoring half a nation's brainpower greatly diminishes competitiveness, culminating in a weak economy. The same principle applies to the segment of the male population that grows up in poverty with few educational options.

Nations in the OECD, an organization of thirty-four mostly wealthy countries, invest, on average, 0.6 percent of GDP each year for job training and other work preparation programs.[3] These efforts are intended to help workers displaced by new technologies transition to a new job. The United States spends just 0.1 percent of GDP to aid our unemployed workers. The changing demands of the workplace require workers with cutting-edge skills. The frustration faced by many unemployed Americans could be ameliorated by providing additional educational opportunities. Without sufficient investment in education and training, the number of unemployed individuals will increase.

As established work habits become obsolete, employees must adjust to new challenges. Young people graduating from college will not be prepared for a lifetime job in our modern economy. There will be a need for career-focused educational training throughout an employee's lifetime. A practical and cost-effective method might be to have companies require each employee to participate in a two- or three-week skill-renewal program each year. Workers would be paid to gain knowledge and acquire new skills designated by the employer. Proficiency tests would be given to each employee to encourage diligent participation. Performance meeting reasonable standards would be required.

RECRUITING TALENTED TEACHERS

Educators who produce successful entrepreneurs and skilled workers are of great value to our society. There is nothing more valuable in the classroom than a clever, proficient teacher. Why should the average MD, who spends most of his or her time writing prescriptions, be paid two to three times as much as a top-notch teacher? The classroom skill needed to convey complex concepts and encourage rational thinking is as least as challenging as the expertise needed to diagnose and treat common physical ailments.

Some people have a natural aptitude for teaching. William James once said, "When all is said and done, the fact remains that some teachers have a naturally inspiring presence, and can make their exercises interesting, while others simply cannot."[4] Identifying young people with pedagogical potential and encouraging them to become teachers should be a top priority. The best and the brightest should be properly compensated to keep them in the classroom. Investing in human capital improves our schools more than expenditures on impressive buildings and athletic facilities.

ENLIGHTENED MANAGEMENT

Informed leadership in our schools is vital. School principals should be trained to apply the same management principles that have been effective in the private sector. These include clear goals for teachers, systematic performance tracking, and the availability of financial incentives for superior instructors. The essential ingredient is hiring and training talented teachers who provide rigorous lessons and who believe that all of their students can excel.

Paying teachers based on the number of years on the job does not provide an incentive for improving instructional outcomes. There are sensible methods for examining outcomes in the classroom to assess effectiveness. Management should have the option of promoting those who can teach and demoting or firing those who can't. Salaries are the primary expense of public education. If a teacher is not effective, the money is wasted.

TEACHERS' UNIONS

The dominance of teachers' unions is a problem. Unions have resisted reforms that are needed to improve our schools. Tying the hands of a principal with a union contract that prevents the removal of an ineffective teacher is detrimental for an entire classroom of children. Teachers, like the other members of humanity, generally perform more proficiently when appropriate workplace incentives are operative. Collective bargaining is often more concerned with employee benefits than with enhancing educational outcomes. Our children are harmed by employment contracts that provide job security in the absence of demonstrated proficiency. The rise of charter schools has been the direct result of the public's awareness that union control has often had negative consequences.

Many individuals of a liberal persuasion have bemoaned the ineffectiveness of inner-city and rural public schools at the same time they have pandered to teachers' unions and underperforming teachers. Market-oriented citizens presume that voucher schemes for privately managed schools would provide more effective educational experiences for our children. Recent evidence would seem to indicate that private versus public may not be the key issue. While charter schools in Boston, New Orleans, and New York City have improved outcomes for children in impoverished neighborhoods, other charter efforts elsewhere with less capable management have outcomes that are no better or sometimes worse than public schools.

INNOVATIVE PUBLIC SCHOOL OPTIONS

Charter schools are not the only option for families that cannot afford the cost of a private school. In several urban areas, parents are given choices among a number of public schools. Sometimes curriculum diversity is offered, such as foreign language immersion or Montessori teaching methods. In San Francisco, parents can select several dozen schools among the seventy-five available elementary schools, rank these according to their preferences, and then enter their prospective student in a complex, computerized lottery system.[5] If there are more requests for a particular school than openings, the system places students in their highest-ranked school based on their lottery positions and some complex tie-breaker rules (e.g., siblings in that school, neighborhood proximity, and other factors). Once a student receives an assignment, his or her preference choices for unselected schools are released, providing an opportunity for other students to receive a new assignment that is higher on their preference list.

An advantage of this system is that school administrators receive empirical feedback regarding which schools are performing well and which ones are not. Schools that are low on parent preference choices are ones that need better management. Schools that are failing can be targeted for revitalization.

EFFECTIVE TEACHING

Research over the past several decades has highlighted the teaching techniques that are most productive. Practical training can be helpful, especially opportunities for teacher collaboration and mentoring. Schools also need to provide tutoring for students who are falling behind. Well-organized classroom discussions have been shown to augment problem solving and solution development. Often longer school days and longer terms can help. Both South Korea and Finland have been leaders in enhancing educational programs. Much can be learned from their pioneering endeavors.

With modern computer equipment for regular testing, pupil progress can be followed. The development of more online courses and other out-of-the-classroom learning opportunities augments traditional teaching methods with new tools based on computer technology. Automating lectures and testing protocols reduces cost, increases availability, and allows students to learn at their own pace.

It would also be helpful if our public schools made curriculum modifications that are appropriate for our modern society. For more than sixty years, scientists have known that there is a critical period in child development when language learning occurs rapidly. Children between ages four and twelve acquire language skills effortlessly. As students age, they apparently lose the ability to hear and pronounce subtle aspects of our planet's many languages. Many schools still begin foreign language training in high school. This is far from optimal. Our global economy requires workers who are fluent in languages other than English. Foreign language learning should be introduced in grammar school if not before. Some schools currently provide language-immersion learning beginning in prekindergarten classes and continuing through elementary school.

Another improvement would be to enrich the mathematics curriculum. Currently there is a focus on concepts that have practical value primarily for engineers and other technical workers. Few of our children are likely to become rocket scientists. Most will need, however, a firm grasp of arithmetic and logical thinking. Many of our young people could benefit from courses in logic, probability theory, and statistical reasoning. These courses should be available in high school. Gaining mathematical insights and concepts that are relevant to everyday life would enhance the intellectual arsenal of all citizens. Course offerings in financial planning and investment strategies should also be available.

Our understanding of the world has advanced over the past two centuries primarily because we have employed scientific reasoning. It is common for people to support established beliefs by selectively citing data that are consistent with those beliefs. Positive examples are not sufficient to prove an idea is correct. Science advances by generating testable hypotheses, systematically collecting relevant observations, and determining whether the evidence is consistent with the premise. Theories that survive multiple tests by individuals attempting to disprove them tend to gain support. Science does not prove the correctness of ideas. Instead it accepts an idea until further analysis provides a better interpretation of the facts. High school students would profit from an introduction to evidence-based reasoning, the essence of the scientific method.

Employees would be more productive workers if their decisions were based on logical reasoning and empirical data instead of rigid beliefs or emotional biases. The common fallacies of human thinking have been thoughtfully discussed by Nobel Prize–winning author Daniel Kahneman in his *New York Times* bestseller, *Thinking, Fast and Slow* (Farrar, Straus and Giroux, 2011). Students would benefit from exposure to these ideas and concepts. Learning how to make rational decisions in real-world settings would be an excellent exercise for young people preparing to join the nation's workforce.

An educational issue that has been the source of much disagreement is whether Darwinian evolution should be taught in our schools. Many Americans have a problem with teachers covering a topic that may be inconsistent with biblical doctrine. Exposure to Darwin does not mean that children have to accept what they hear. Being familiar with the theory of evolution, however, permits our children to discuss biology in an informed manner.

The biology curriculum would also benefit from more emphasis on human physiology. Understanding how the heart and lungs function, what happens in the digestive system, and how our musculature reacts to exercise would be useful information. Discussions of the benefits of sensible nutrition and aerobic activity might be more meaningful to young people if classroom recommendations were integrated with knowledge of how our bodies function. The current epidemic of obesity might be reduced if children learned about the hazards of eating junk food and avoiding physical exercise within the context of how these undesirable behaviors affect our bodies. A field trip to the school cafeteria to become familiar with healthy protocols for food preparation would also be a beneficial addition to the biology curriculum. In addition, encouraging physical education programs that provide a broad range of options for aerobic exercise would be helpful.

Our high school students score below their international competitors in understanding science. The most recent Programme for International

Student Assessment, an international test of science, math, and reading skills of fifteen-year-old students, appraises the effectiveness of American public schools.[6] The results are not encouraging. The average math scores of Singaporean teens are three years ahead of our teens. American students' math and science scores are also below the level of students in Japan, South Korea, Canada, Finland, and Estonia. To be competitive in a global economy and to vote intelligently in elections in which technology and science policy are increasingly more important, our young people need improved classroom instruction.

Leadership from Washington has done little to enhance relevant educational coursework. For more than a decade, scientists have been concerned with the impending risks posed by climate change. Legislators in our nation's capital have ignored these warnings and many have even denied the existence of a potential problem. As other nations have moved away from energy acquired from fossil fuels, Americans have been tardy in recognizing that carbon dioxide and other pollutants are a serious issue. Perhaps with more emphasis on science education, the next generation of leaders will provide legislation addressing the environmental realities of our evolving planet.

It would also be valuable for our school systems to cover an old-fashioned topic: civics. Every school child should understand the basic structure and functioning of our government. Our ability to keep and defend our liberty depends on an informed electorate. If our citizens are to elect representatives who provide insightful leadership, our educational system must provide literacy, foster the ability to think logically, and impart an appreciation of communitarian principles.

The Founding Fathers were well aware of this necessity. In George Washington's words, "A primary object should be the education of our youth in the science of government. In a republic, what species of knowledge can be equally important? And what duty more pressing than communicating it to those who are to be the future guardians of the liberties of the country?"[7]

Thomas Jefferson amplified this idea: "I know of no safe depository of the ultimate powers of society but the people themselves; and if we think them not enlightened enough to exercise their control with a wholesome discretion, the remedy is not to take it from them but to inform their discretion by education. This is the true corrective of abuses of Constitutional power."[8] James Madison also believed that understanding how our government works is essential, writing that "a well-instructed people alone can be permanently a free people."[9]

THE IMPORTANCE OF EDUCATIONAL OPPORTUNITY

J. D. Vance's *Hillbilly Elegy: A Memoir of a Family and Culture in Crisis* (HarperCollins, 2016) provides an example of how educational opportunity can change a young person's life. Vance was born into a culture common in Kentucky's coal country. He describes his ancestors as people who "would rather shoot you than argue with you." His family left Kentucky in the 1940s and settled in southwestern Ohio, where his grandfather worked in a steel plant.

His mother was a poor role model, abusing drugs and alcohol while entertaining a parade of male companions. Vance described the lessons he learned from his mother in colorful language: "Never speak at a reasonable volume when screaming will do"; "it's okay to slap and punch"; "always express your feelings in a way that's insulting and hurtful to your partner."

In recent years, job prospects have worsened for young men in blue-collar factory towns. Unlike many of his contemporaries, Vance did not turn to alcohol or drugs. Instead, he joined the Marines and subsequently graduated from Ohio State and Yale Law School. What accounts for this surprising transformation? He was fortunate to have grandparents and an older sister who encouraged his educational studies and provided some stability in his life.

In addition, there were two essential ingredients to his success. First, he did not blame other people or the government for his situation. "We hillbillies must wake up," he urged. "It starts when we stop blaming Obama or Bush or faceless companies and ask ourselves what we can do to make things better." He took responsibility for his own life and had the grit to take advantage of opportunities when they appeared. The other key ingredient was his commitment to gaining a good education: joining the Marines and then going to college. Today he works in San Francisco at an investment company, is married, and enjoys a lifestyle that many Americans would be happy to emulate. His journey demonstrates that educational opportunity can provide a pathway to the middle class, even for someone who starts with severe handicaps. His rise from poverty is a story that all of us would love to believe is the American norm.

Vance's challenges are not isolated within a few communities in rural America. The lack of educational opportunity also exists in many urban areas. For far too many young people, the zip code in which they live ordains whether or not they will have access to a first-class education. The quality of a child's early schooling heavily influences his or her opportunity to succeed in our market economy. Each child that thrives in the classroom will become a taxpayer instead of maturing into an adult on welfare.

FINANCING PUBLIC EDUCATION

In Europe, the federal governments cover, on average, 50 percent of the cost of primary education. In the US, the federal government covers only 10 percent of the bill. Financing primary education with property taxes leads to very unequal educational opportunities for young people. Additional funding from state sources is also uneven. Vermont provides almost three times as much per child as Utah. Oklahoma, Texas, Kentucky, and Alabama have recently reduced school funding. Children growing up in poor neighborhoods start life with severe educational handicaps.[10] A child that begins the school day without breakfast, with mediocre teachers, and with outdated educational resources is less likely to acquire the knowledge and skills that are needed to compete effectively in a market economy.[11]

An example is the disparity in educational resources in Illinois between Waukegan and Stevenson high schools. These two schools are twenty miles apart, but one spends $18,800 per student and the other allocates only $12,600 per student.[12] The classroom facilities and teachers' salaries reflect this difference. Young people in an impoverished community receive an inferior education. Depending on local property taxes to fund public education selectively handicaps children in less-affluent neighborhoods. Increasing federal investments in K–12 education would help equalize funding. An increase in federal income taxes with a corresponding reduction in local property taxes would level the playing field.

Seniors living in established neighborhoods on limited incomes often face property tax bills that challenge their monetary resources. In some cases, they have to sell the home they have lived in for decades to meet their financial obligations. Additional financing for public schools with federal dollars might permit many of these people to remain in the homes and neighborhoods they love.

The mayor of New York City recently announced a plan to provide free preschool for all of the city's three-year-olds.[13] This initiative could provide early educational instruction for more than sixty thousand children. Florida and Oklahoma have universal, publicly funded preschool for four-year-olds, but the New York City effort for younger children is unusual. Empirical evidence indicates that early education efforts can have a very positive influence on learning outcomes. Focusing on social and emotional development as well as language skills can enhance a young child's success in learning to read.

PERFORMANCE-BASED COLLEGE STIPENDS

We also need new options for financing higher education. A high school diploma is no longer sufficient to prepare young people for a decent job in our technological society. To better prepare these young people to enter the workforce, the federal government could provide stipends for post-secondary education based on school performance. Students that graduate from their high schools in the top third of the class might receive a four-year stipend for college tuition. Students in the second third might receive a two-year stipend for tuition at a community college or a four-year institution. The remaining students might receive a stipend for job training. These funds would be distributed without dependence on neighborhood or regional economic differences. Prospective students would have the option of applying their stipend to the school of their choice. A complex bureaucracy would not be needed to reward young people who perform well in high school or to offer educational opportunities for those students who do less well.

If greater federal funding is provided for college tuition, it would be necessary to determine which educational institutions are eligible to participate. My preference would be to monitor the graduates of each provider, including those with internet-based curriculums, and measure the success of their students in gaining meaningful employment. Educational institutions that perform poorly would be disqualified.

INCOME-SHARING AGREEMENTS

A second innovation would provide an opportunity for students to finance college tuition with a commitment to contribute a percentage of their income after graduation. These income-sharing agreements (ISA) would help a young person attend college without graduating with a huge debt. Repaying by committing 5 percent of each paycheck over a fixed period of time would improve the student's opportunities after college.[14] In contrast to a traditional loan, the student would not have a fixed repayment schedule. He or she would have more career options.

ISA programs could be financed privately or publicly (or through a combination of private and public funds). Private colleges and universities with large endowments might offer ISAs to their own students. By enrolling capable, hardworking young people and providing high-quality education, the institution might actually, over time, provide a better return on their endowment funds than would be received from more conventional investments. Astute administrators at public educational institutions might also make ISA offers that help promising students and protect the taxpayers' interests.

Private individuals could also finance ISAs. Receiving 5 percent of the paycheck from some former students for a fixed number of years may not recoup the lender's investment. However, other former students, those with high-paying jobs, would repay the money borrowed plus a portion of what was borrowed by students who were less financially successful. Since neither the lender nor the borrowers can know in advance who will eventually have the best-paying jobs, the lenders would need to recoup their investments based on the average repayment. A lender who has the foresight to arrange an ISA with a future Bill Gates or Steve Jobs or Elon Musk will not lose money.

The incentives created by this type of arrangement are beneficial for both parties. ISA investors could actively seek students who show promise of future successful employment. Young people from poor neighborhoods who have a high school track record of accomplishment would be likely targets. These individuals are currently less likely to attend college because of financial concerns. Because the lender has skin in the game, he or she would be motivated to help the young student master his or her academic studies. Financing higher education could become more of a market-based process. Students and lenders could work together to seek high-quality, low-cost programs.

As the nature of work changes, employees need to acquire new skills continually. Our colleges and universities should emphasize learning how to learn in addition to specific job skills. New jobs will emerge regularly. Individuals who are adept at learning novel skills throughout their lifetimes will prosper. Search engines on computers and smartphones can provide detailed information on any topic. Educational institutions should emphasize creative thinking, strategic reasoning, and communication skills. The best source for acquiring these abilities might be traditional liberal arts courses.

History demonstrates that our nation has repeatedly overcome new challenges. We cannot avoid being part of the global economy. An attempt to stick our heads in the sand and hope that international competition will go away is futile. If we wish to follow in the footsteps of previous generations, it is time to invest our national resources in a workforce that is more highly skilled than our foreign competitors. Americans should be the ones who design, build, and operate the new machines. The essential ingredient for learning sophisticated skills is education, education, and more education. To be the most powerful economic force on the planet, America needs to create an education system that is second to no other country.

It is an embarrassment that the United States has more offenders in jail in absolute numbers and on a percentage basis than most other nations.[15] European countries average two hundred prisoners for every hundred thousand citizens. In contrast, we incarcerate seven hundred persons for every hundred thousand citizens. We address our failings by locking up the young people whom we have left behind. A recent study discovered that each extra year in prison increases the risk of returning to jail after release by six percentage points. Long prison sentences, especially for young people, produce perennial jailbirds. We spend almost as much taxpayer money on incarcerating criminals as we do on education. It is likely that better education for all our people would increase employment, reduce crime, and help empty our penal institutions. Why not spend more money on education and less money on prisons?

Chapter 7

———

NATIONAL DEFENSE

*What is absurd and monstrous about war is that
men who have no personal quarrel should be
trained to murder one another in cold blood.*
—ALDOUS HUXLEY

There appear to be four major military strategic challenges for the United States. One threat is an attack from an established military power with a plentiful supply of nuclear weapons. A second is the arrival of an invasion force on our Atlantic or Pacific coast, or in Hawaii or Alaska. The third is a terrorist attack from insurgents who have been implanted within our borders. The fourth is hostilities with a rogue nation that has biological and/or nuclear capabilities and is led by an irrational or unpredictable individual. Each of these dangers necessitates appropriate defensive preparations by our nation.

In determining how to invest military funds, our leaders should perform a means-ends evaluation of the most effective defensive strategies. Technological innovations continue to alter what we might face in a future confrontation. Our equipment and strategies should be tailored to address future military battle conditions.

DEFENSE AGAINST NUCLEAR WARHEADS

The threat of a nuclear exchange between major world powers has been present for six decades. The absence of this horrific event is a combination of good fortune and each nation's concern that initiating a nuclear strike would produce a reprisal strike. There is a high probability that both nations would be utterly destroyed. This anticipated sequence, known as mutually assured destruction, has kept nuclear weapons under wraps. The United States has developed a powerful triad of delivery systems that virtually guarantees that an attacker could not avoid massive retaliation. We have the capability to deliver nuclear warheads launched from submarines, from land-based missile silos, and from stealthy attack aircraft. To avoid a nuclear attack by a major power, we must discourage potential aggression by maintaining our threat of massive retaliation.

The United States has also made major investments in deterrence. The Patriot solid-fuel rocket has medium-range antiballistic missile capability. This projectile is radar-guided and has homing capability as it approaches its target. It is employed near urban and military targets to destroy incoming warheads.

The United States continues to develop novel defensive weapons that are expected to be more capable than the Patriot missile. Our military is currently developing an innovative cannon called the railgun. It employs electromagnetic energy to accelerate a projectile that can be guided to its target. The railgun cartridge gains speed as it travels the length of a 32-foot barrel, exiting the muzzle at 1.25 miles per second. It has a range of approximately 100 miles and destroys the target by penetration with the vast kinetic energy of its momentum. The railgun requires a tremendous amount of electrical power and is thus appropriate for land-based installations or for duty on a naval ship with high-energy capability. When perfected, the railgun should be extremely effective against incoming intercontinental ballistic missiles and anti-ship projectiles.

Our nation is also working on high-energy lasers. The functionality of these devices depends on power requirements. The most powerful versions, 150-kilowatt lasers, would be effective against incoming missiles and aircraft. The advantage of these weapons is their low cost per shot (a few dollars) and their incredible speed (a laser travels at the speed of light). They can disable enemy attackers at a distance by melting key electronic control equipment and can destroy them at a closer range by igniting fuel and munitions. A laser weapon would be highly effective against an enemy attack involving a large number of warheads (i.e., a swarm attack).

DEFENSE AGAINST AN INVADING ARMY

It is highly unlikely that a hostile nation would attempt to land military forces on our Atlantic or Pacific coasts. Our surveillance capability with satellites and drones makes it virtually impossible for another nation to invade our territory without early detection. The intruders would be decimated by our Air Force and Navy long before they could successfully place troops on our soil. Our current aerial and naval capabilities should discourage any such effort in the foreseeable future.

Even in the unlikely event that an enemy could overcome our professional military forces by placing troops on American soil, the challenge of holding territory would be a nightmare for any occupier. The presence of three hundred million firearms in America along with modern hunting and tracking gear would be a challenge for any invader planning to establish a foothold here. Civilians are no match for a modern army, but their presence would probably be a significant irritant.

TERRORIST ATTACKS

Our country has established an internal security organization that works in conjunction with federal and local police to detect and disable threats from lone-wolf individuals and terrorist organizations. These efforts need to be refined to maximize protection for our citizenry. Our country should also train special military forces to provide immediate assistance when terrorist activity has been detected.

The primary challenge is identifying potential perpetrators before they can launch an attack. This requires electronic surveillance, cooperation from private citizens, and sharing of vital information among governmental agencies. Once a plot has been discovered, our country has adequate means to detain, interrogate, and incarcerate the offenders.

Although media coverage and political debate have focused public attention on the dangers of terrorist attacks, these events have been infrequent.[1] From 1995 through 2014, terrorists have been responsible for an average of 158 deaths per year. Most of these (2,996) occurred on September 11, 2001. For comparison, the number of homicides from 2010 through 2013 averaged approximately 12,000 per year. Deaths caused by auto accidents averaged 33,652 per year between 2011 and 2015. Between 2004 and 2013, the number of deaths from lightning strikes averaged 33 per year. In this same period, the deaths from encounters with terrorists have averaged 4 per year. Most of these perpetrators were homegrown offenders rather than immigrants or embedded foreigners.

There is a significant danger that a small cell of terrorists could detonate a truck bomb or employ chemical or biological weapons. There are also serious threats that do not require extensive preparation or technical skill, such as setting wildfires or breaching earthen dams. A single attack of this type could produce mass casualties. To meet these threats, it is essential that our security forces maintain a high level of preparedness to prevent these events. If such an event does occur, despite our best efforts to prevent it, we must be ready to react quickly to provide medical support and anything else that can help save lives.

The likelihood that an American citizen will die at the hands of a terrorist, however, is about the same as the likelihood that he or she will win a multimillion-dollar lottery. The number of deaths in the United States due to terrorism since the September 11, 2001, attack is fewer than the number of deaths from falling off a ladder or down stairs. Our country has spent billions of dollars of taxpayer money in an effort to stamp out these dreadful events. The reality is that these attacks, especially the lone-wolf type, are very difficult to detect. Although it is essential that we maintain a robust capability to uncover and combat terror attacks, placing equal emphasis on the prevention of gun homicides and automobile collisions would probably save many more lives.

ROGUE NATIONS

Countries controlled by religious fanatics or demagogues who place little value on the lives of their countrymen might attack us or one of our allies despite the virtual guarantee of colossal destruction and loss of life in their homeland. If and when such an existential threat appears, our nation should have the capability to take defensive action by eliminating that threat. Responding after a deranged dictator envelops New York or San Francisco in a mushroom cloud is not an acceptable plan.

When a rogue nation becomes a malignant cancer and diplomacy fails, world leaders should consider an effort to eliminate its political and military leaders. Regime change by decapitation is a more sensible approach than mounting a major military invasion. Instead of destroying infrastructure and killing young soldiers, the objective should be to terminate the individuals who pose the threat. Satellite and drone surveillance with human agents on the ground could locate and target key facilities. With conventional weapons, a major power or a coalition of democratic nations could surgically remove the country's leaders and critical military facilities. The arrival of several cruise missiles, without warning, could eliminate the people intent on developing and using lethal war materials to attack our nation. Intercontinental rockets with nuclear warheads are a serious threat that should not be ignored when the individuals in command are mentally unstable or potentially delusional.

An apt analogy is Rudyard Kipling's "Rikki-Tikki-Tavi" story in *The Jungle Book*.[2] Rikki-Tikki-Tavi, a pet mongoose, protects a British family living in India from the danger posed by two cobras. The mongoose is a small, highly strung mammal that attacks snakes by approaching sufficiently close to provoke a strike. The mongoose dodges the snake's thrust and attacks the snake's head. With a single bite, it kills the snake.

Kipling's narration is an allegory for humanity's frequent confrontations with menacing intruders. The cobras serve as an existential threat to the British family. The mongoose has an innate understanding of the danger. Rather than wait until one of the cobras attacks and kills a child, Rikki-Tikki-Tavi deals with the impending danger without delay. In contrast to human leaders, who often react only after a devastating strike has occurred, the mongoose recognized the peril and took action.

The second aspect of interest is the mongoose's plan of battle. Instead of engaging in a long, drawn-out fight involving damage to the house or garden, Rikki-Tikki-Tavi focuses his attack on the essential target, the central command unit, the cobra's head. Humans have often settled their differences by building formidable armies that clash with great loss of life and tremendous destruction to urban areas. Maybe Kipling's children's story captures a useful strategy for dealing with a terrible threat. A preemptive attack that removes the leadership of a rogue nation might avoid a future devastating war.

Another relevant analogy is the method a chess grandmaster employs when competing with an opponent of lesser skill. Instead of fighting a war of attrition, attempting to win by gradually reducing the opponent's piece count, the chess grandmaster unleashes a direct attack on the king of the weaker player. The contest is ended with most of the chess pieces still on the playing field. The pawns and knights survive the battle. Only the king pays the ultimate price.

There is historical evidence that preemptive actions can be effective in displacing a direct threat to the national security of a nation.[3] During the latter half of the twentieth century, Israel's secret service employed targeted assassinations to remove enemy agents who aspired to destroy the emergent Israeli nation. Meir Dagan, chief of the Mossad, believed that open warfare should only be used as a last resort, when there was no other option. He believed that the use of assassination was more ethical than waging a war in which the lives of young soldiers and civilians of all ages would be terminated.

In July 1956, Israel's leadership decided to remove two individuals who were organizing and financing terrorist attacks on citizens of their newborn nation. Colonel Mustafa Hafez, an officer in the Egyptian military intelligence, and Salah Mustafa, the Egyptian military attaché in Jordan, were both assassinated. These clandestine actions of the Mossad were effective in reducing the number of terrorist incursions into Israel.

In October of the same year, Israel's intelligence officers learned that Egypt, Jordan, and Syria were planning a land invasion of the Sinai Peninsula. They also interdicted communications indicating that the Egyptian General Staff, who were meeting with their counterparts in Syria, would be returning to Egypt on October 28. A single fighter plane was dispatched to take advantage of this information. This aircraft intercepted the Egyptian Ilyushin and attacked with twenty-millimeter cannons, converting the plane transporting the Egyptian military leaders into a flaming chunk of wreckage. The ensuing chaos contributed to Israel's military victory in the war that began the next day. Victory in the Sinai campaign gave Israel eleven years of relative peace to bolster their military capacity. This interlude was probably a major factor in preparing Israel for the Six-Day War in 1967.

When Syrian, Egyptian, and Jordanian troops massed on Israel's borders early in June 1967, the country's leaders were convinced that the Arab states were intending to destroy the State of Israel once and forever. To meet this threat, on June 5, the entire Israeli air force launched a preemptive attack on enemy airfields, destroying in a matter of minutes almost all of their adversaries' combat airplanes. With control of the skies over the battlefields, the Israeli army routed the would-be attackers. The Arab intention to obliterate Israel crumbled in six days. Once again, preemptive action aimed at disrupting the enemy's military objectives prevented hostile neighbors from annihilating Israel.

This approach, asymmetric warfare, is a significant departure from our own country's current defense strategy. Striking another nation without a declaration of war has few precedents in US military history. Decapitating the leadership and destroying the military assets of a rogue nation in a preemptive fashion, however, would seem to be preferable to other defensive options. Mounting a full-scale conventional invasion is costly in equipment and lives. One wonders why young people should be killed and cities destroyed to remove an existential threat. Regime change by decapitation and targeted destruction of offensive weaponry would be preferable for the international community and especially for the citizens of the rogue nation.

The plan would be to remove the head of state and his or her top military advisors. Simultaneously disabling the enemy's communication infrastructure and "blinding" its radar equipment would heighten confusion. Subsequent attacks on military installations using cruise missiles and stealth air power would limit damage to our forces and neighboring allies.

Our country should have no interest in gaining territory or taking political control of the rogue nation. Restructuring the nation's leadership after the attack could be left to local officials with cooperation from neighboring countries and the United Nations. Conducting a mission of this type, including financial aid to help establish a new national government, would cost much less than the two trillion dollars we have expended on our invasion of Iraq. In comparison to a military invasion, a surgical surprise strike would save lives, leave local political organizations intact, and retain most of the transportation and commercial infrastructure. The outcome would be more favorable for both our country and the inhabitants of the country we attacked.

One can wonder if the current disaster in Syria and the resulting massive migration of families from the Middle East into Europe could have been avoided by an unannounced attack on the Syrian leadership in 2014. This would have reduced human casualties and the destruction of the country's infrastructure. A decisive surgical attack would have been preferable to the horror and devastation that has subsequently taken place.

The current Supreme leader of North Korea, Kim Jong-un, allocates 22 percent of his county's financial resources to military expenditures, including an army of 1.2 million soldiers.[4] This compares to his neighbor, South Korea, where 3 percent of GDP is spent on an army of 650,000 soldiers. North Korea's per capita GDP is approximately $1,800 per year. This figure for South Korea is $32,400 per year. North Korea has severe shortages of food and personal amenities and a political system that appears to be a police state. Kim Jong-un is marshaling his technical and military resources to develop nuclear-tipped intercontinental ballistic missiles. Experts predict that he has the current capability of launching a nuclear attack on his neighbors and soon will be able to attack the United States.

North Korea would appear to have little reason to be concerned about an invasion by a foreign power. Neither South Korea nor Japan has the military capability, and the United States has no reason to attack a non-belligerent North Korea. In addition, China, on North Korea's border, would not want to have a democratic, capitalistic nation as its neighbor and would therefore be likely to actively defend North Korea. Kim Jong-un does not need nuclear weapons for deterrence since he has sufficient conventional military weapons to decimate Seoul and more than a million soldiers who could defend his territory.

Given these realities, it is surprising that the leadership of North Korea is currently making major investments in nuclear-tipped, long-range missiles, purportedly for defensive reasons. This would seem to be particularly irrational given the degree of poverty and hunger experienced by a large segment of the population. Why is North Korea placing a high priority on developing offensive military weapons? The objective would seem to be the development of a capability to threaten neighbors with nuclear destruction.

Given Kim Jong-un's emphasis on offensive military weapons, he is creating an existential threat to the United States and its allies. Should we stand by while he bullies or invades his neighbors or, worse yet, makes a preemptive strike on the United States? Should we take action only if North Korea devastates a major American metropolitan area? If so, our historical role of protecting allies and thus preserving peace on the planet would be severely compromised.

A preemptive military action eliminating the leaders of a rogue nation who threaten the peaceful coexistence of neighboring states might also provide an object lesson to the leaders of other rogue regimes. The willingness of demagogues and religious fanatics to threaten democratic nations might be greatly reduced. In addition, these nations might be less inclined to organize and finance terrorist attacks.

UNMANNED WEAPONS PLATFORMS

There is a common tendency among military organizations to make extensive preparations to fight the previous war. When Germany invaded Poland in 1939, Polish officers on horseback charged the German armored vehicles with the intention of overcoming these military weapons with small arms. The outcome was predictable and unfortunate for Poland. The pace of technology moves forward much more rapidly in the twenty-first century. Military equipment and battle strategies that once were effective are no longer viable. Building military forces with outdated equipment and outdated strategic thinking is a recipe for disaster.

Our ability to detect military activity anywhere on the planet greatly reduces the threat of an unexpected attack. A surprise air assault on Hawaii, such as happened during the Second World War, would not be possible today. In addition, "eyes in the sky" also make large troop concentrations a military liability. Once detected, troop concentrations become vulnerable targets for devastating, high-tech weapons. Without forewarning, a large area can be blanketed with small bomblets that destroy both people and machines. Victory is no longer assured by a nation that maintains a large army. Technological sophistication dominates numerical supremacy in troop deployments. A dozen highly trained special-force soldiers can provide GPS information and laser targeting. With this reconnaissance, our military can employ modern weaponry capable of destroying heavily defended fortifications and massive troop concentrations.

Tomorrow's wars will be fought with machines controlled by servicepeople located in fixed bunkers or in mobile control centers. Military battles will be conducted with unmanned aerial and ground-based weapons platforms. Fifth-generation military aircraft, such as the F-22 Raptor or the latest F-35 air-superiority fighter, will be replaced with unmanned aircraft controlled remotely by operators hundreds of miles distant from the site of action. These sixth-generation aircraft will be faster, lighter, stealthier, and more maneuverable than their predecessors.[5] Without a human pilot, these craft will be capable of radical changes in direction that would cause a pilot to black out. In addition, they will provide an option to attack targets at a greater distance from the launch point since unmanned aerial vehicles need not make a return trip home. Without support equipment for the pilot, these planes will also be less expensive to build.

An additional advantage of these aerial weapons will be the opportunity to mount a swarm attack on a high-value, heavily defended target without loss of our pilots' lives. A coordinated attack of several dozen unmanned aerial weapons platforms, even with substantial losses, is likely to achieve the mission objective. Only a few attack aircraft need to unload weapons on the target in order to conclude a successful mission.

On the ground, unmanned mobile weapons platforms will also be controlled from a distance. The new battlefield tank will be smaller and lighter with less armor. These modifications will not compromise its battlefield effectiveness. Some of these will be tracked vehicles like our current tanks. Others will be six-legged weapon platforms for rugged terrain. At sea, unmanned undersea robotic agents will engage in dangerous missions to clear mines, distribute sensors, collect information regarding enemy activity, and, if needed, directly attack enemy vessels. These military platforms will be relatively inexpensive and therefore can be employed in large numbers with the capability of making swarm attacks.

In the air, on land, and at sea, these unmanned vehicles will have dual guidance capabilities. The most common mode will be direct control by a team of operators. There would be a surveillance officer, a weapons specialist, and a pilot or driver. If the communication link were to fail or be interrupted by enemy action, the weapons platform would switch to autonomous mode. It would employ GPS information and intelligent software to approach and attack its designated target. Machines feel no pain, lack empathy for the pain of others, and will follow orders without exception until they are destroyed. They are not the type of opponent a human would wish to meet on the battlefield.

At sea, our naval forces will need reconfiguration. Large ships, such as aircraft carriers, will be difficult to defend against a massed assault. Many small enemy ships, each launching multiple ship-to-ship missiles in a near simultaneous attack, would present a formidable problem. Even if we could destroy most of the enemy projectiles, it is likely that some would reach their target. The Rand Corporation recently conducted an analysis of the effectiveness of a swarm attack as described earlier and concluded that the advantage would rest with the enemy. Our aircraft carriers, in order to survive, would have to remain far out to sea with an opportunity to destroy attackers before they were within missile range. This, of course, would compromise the effectiveness of the aircraft carrier. Planes would burn a substantial amount of fuel before reaching their target. Consequently, their time for action at their destination would be limited.

Our future naval force should be less dependent on aircraft-carrier armadas and more focused on distributed forces, such as smaller ships capable of launching cruise missiles and unmanned aircraft. Our Navy's newest and largest-ever destroyer, the USS *Zumwalt*, is so stealthy that its radar image is indistinguishable from a small fishing boat.[6] Without a pilot aboard, an aerial weapons platform such as the F-35B, with vertical takeoff capability, could be dispatched from this vessel close to enemy shores. The F-35 can talk directly to the *Zumwalt* and direct ship-launched missiles to enemy targets. The sophisticated electronics on the F-35 are also capable of coordinating drone surveillance and attack missions over enemy territory.

After unloading its weapons, an unmanned drone would have the option of making a kamikaze dive on an enemy target. It could also return to the launching vehicle for refitting, refueling, and preparation for its next mission. The naval vessel, several sixth-generation F-35Bs, and a support crew would be vastly less expensive than an aircraft carrier, less vulnerable to adversary attacks, and might be as effective in accomplishing our military objectives.

Our navy also has destroyer-size ships capable of launching manned vertical takeoff and landing craft, such as the MV-22 Osprey.[7] This helicopter-airplane hybrid can fly at speeds in excess of 300 mph and carry up to fifteen tons of cargo or thirty-two troops or a mixture of the two. A relatively small, stealthy ship under the cover of darkness could insert a small, well-equipped force into enemy territory. With appropriate communication and battlefield gear, these soldiers would have the capability of locating and "lighting up" high-value targets for cruise missiles or other guided weapons.

This type of surreptitious special-force insertion would be significantly aided by taking down enemy radar defenses and communication equipment. Combat aircraft can fire electromagnetic pulses with pinpoint accuracy to target individual buildings, blacking out electronics rather than destroying physical structures. The use of this technology would precede the arrival of our attack force. The opportunity for an enemy to detect our intrusion, to communicate information, and to take defensive action would be extremely limited. From the opponent's perspective, the failure of their electronic equipment would initially be considered a computer glitch. Our military operations could be concluded before the rogue nation was aware that something was amiss.

The Textron V-247 Vigilant drone is another weapon with tilt-rotor engines that provides vertical liftoff capability.[8] This is a large drone (with a 65-foot wingspan) capable of sustained flight (eleven hours) at 300 knots without refueling. It has a combat range of 450 nautical miles and can carry MK-50 anti-submarine torpedoes, Hellfire missiles, and Joint Air-to-Ground Missiles. It can take off from and land on Arleigh Burke–class destroyers. This large drone provides significant new capabilities in unmanned naval weaponry.

The skill sets needed by our soldiers in a future encounter will be quite different from the attributes required for effective soldiers in previous wars. Tomorrow's soldiers will operate intricate technical equipment. Physical strength and athletic prowess, for most soldiers, will be unnecessary. Sending large groups of American soldiers into traditional battlefield encounters essentially squanders our technical advantages in air power and intelligence gathering. Military battles will be won by the nation with superior technology and with personnel properly trained to use it.

We will still need highly trained, superbly equipped, and physically capable soldiers. These elite troops will operate within small units that are organized with a range of skills that would augment the capabilities of the unit. They would often operate behind enemy lines, providing information unavailable from satellites or surveillance drones. Human intelligence often provides valuable information unavailable from mechanical systems. An additional mission for these troops would be to mastermind the action of our unmanned weapons platforms. Most of the time, these soldiers would orchestrate the battlefield without engaging directly. On a few occasions, they would need to be prepared for direct action, such as rescuing hostages or eliminating high-value enemy personnel. It might be necessary to repeat the type of mission that eradicated Osama bin Laden.

Success in a future war will be heavily dependent on our ability to intercept, disrupt, and "defang" enemy communications and to "blind" their sensors. Our own command and control technology must be impervious to enemy hackers. A successful aerial attack will require stealthy approaches by aircraft or naval vessels that launch missiles a considerable distance from the intended target. These missiles will fly at supersonic speeds, avoiding detection by hugging the terrain below the vision of the enemy's radar. Our objective will be the destruction of the enemy's detection devices and airfields before they can respond. Rather than battle hostile aircraft in the skies, we should destroy them on the ground before our incursions are discovered. Engaging in manned aerial attacks over enemy territory would be as foolish as attacking armored battle tanks with soldiers mounted on horseback.

Our battle strategy should avoid troop concentrations. Why make our soldiers targets for the horrendous damage of modern weaponry? Elite training and human courage are no longer sufficient. In 2016, General Mark Milley, the Army Chief of Staff, anticipated a fundamental change in ground warfare. The battlefield will be "highly lethal," unlike previous wars. Milley observed that long-range precision weapons will be able to "hammer big, obvious targets," creating a necessity to disperse "into small units moving independently with no semblance of a front line."[9]

Our military should face enemy fire with machines rather than soldiers.[10] Let the robots fight and die. They don't have spouses or children. They will not need years of treatment to repair physical impairment after the war is over. Our goal would be to save lives and reduce the medical challenges faced by our Veterans Administration. Future wars should be fought with mechanical forces. May the best machines win, and hopefully they will be our machines.

───────

The United States currently has approximately thirteen thousand military aircraft. In comparison, China and Russia, the world's next-largest aerial powers, have a total of only two thousand to three thousand military aircraft each.[11] We currently have 1.5 million military personnel on active duty. There is no real advantage of training and equipping a large number of soldiers when our strategic goals do not require military actions that involve large troop deployments. This number of personnel is probably much larger than what would be needed in the future to man, control, and service our war machines.

Given these observations and analysis, it is fair to ask whether our current military posture makes sense. Do we really need 1.5 million military personnel on active duty? Maintaining a fleet of thirteen thousand military aircraft, most of which are of limited value in a modern war, would seem to be an investment with little return value. Our country should have no desire to acquire territory or treasure by invading our neighbors or nations overseas. Our defensive obligations require a modified force structure. We should invest more in technology and less in personnel. It would be feasible to create a dominant military force that consisted of only half a million military personnel. This would be an elite force operating with modern technology.

Recalibrating the size of our military forces would put a lot of people out of work. We could avoid a transition that creates unemployment by funding major improvements in our country's infrastructure.

Resurfacing and building roads, repairing and constructing bridges, modernizing rail transport, adding new airports and new harbors, and implementing other new transportation technologies will require many workers. These improvements would also make our businesses more efficient and thus more competitive in the global economy. It would also reduce traffic snarls each morning and decrease carbon emissions and other sources of pollution. With a stronger economy, there will also be additional non-construction jobs.

Restructuring our military forces will be difficult. Politicians resist closing military bases in their home districts. Repeated recommendations by the Pentagon have been routinely disregarded. Shouldn't legislators place more emphasis on sharpening our military capabilities than gaining personal political advantage by retaining local superfluous facilities at unnecessary taxpayer expense?

Chapter 8

TAXATION AND RESOURCE ALLOCATION

The hardest thing in the world to understand is the income tax.

—ALBERT EINSTEIN

Our representatives in Washington should manage the country's financial resources in a way that balances income and expenditures. But the government continues to spend more than it collects. The recent tax cuts orchestrated by the Trump administration are expected to annually increase our national debt by more than one trillion dollars.[1] These deficits are not sustainable. Eventually, the interest payments on our debt will dominate federal expenditures. We should be paying down our debt in years when the economy is strong and reserve borrowing for the inevitable times when our economy is in a recession. Any plan to reorganize government taxation and expenditures needs to bring the two in balance over the long term.

The federal government spent $3.7 trillion in 2015. These expenditures included $882 billion for Social Security (24 percent), $937 billion for health care (25 percent), $583 billion for defense (16 percent), $479 billion for other mandatory programs such as food stamps and unemployment insurance (13 percent), and $223 billion on interest payments on the national debt (6 percent). Discretionary spending represented 16 percent of the total, amounting to $585 billion.[2]

Federal revenues in 2015 were $3.2 trillion, a difference between income and spending of $500 billion. The sources of government revenue were personal income taxes ($1.5 trillion), corporate taxes ($342 billion), Social Security contributions ($1.1 trillion), excise taxes ($96 billion), and various other sources ($195 billion).[3]

In the 2016 presidential election, neither major-party candidate offered a proposal to address this problem. In his acceptance speech at the party convention, the Republican nominee, the "change candidate," promised to increase funding for our military, spend one trillion dollars to enhance the nation's transportation infrastructure, reduce taxes for everyone, and balance the budget. This "Alice in Wonderland" budget proposal is typical of the way our elected representatives have been addressing the national deficit for many years.

Donald Trump, in the 2016 campaign for president, also frequently stated that the United States is the highest-taxed country in the world. In fact, this assertion is counterfactual. The Organisation for Economic Co-operation and Development (OECD) in 2014 made an assessment of the overall tax burden for each of its thirty-five member nations.[4] The nations with the highest tax burden as a percentage of GDP were Denmark (49.6 percent), France (45.5 percent), Belgium (45 percent), Finland (43.8 percent), and Italy (43.7 percent). The tax burden calculated for the United States was 25.9 percent. Of the thirty-five nations in the OECD, the United States ranked thirty-second. Only three countries—South Korea, Chile, and Mexico—had a lower tax burden. Our country is a low-tax nation. If the United States maintained its current level of spending and taxed its citizens at the average rate of the OECD members (34.2 percent), our national debt would be eliminated within a few years.

FALLING BEHIND

In the United States, our legislators have not prioritized expenditures on education, an investment that is desperately needed to ensure our future economic competitiveness. They have also cut back funding for infrastructure. Budget allocations for roads, bridges, airports, harbors, and other conveyance facilities have been insufficient to maintain a first-class transportation system.[5] Recent rating data indicate that roads rated poor or worse for bumpiness increased from 16 percent in 2005 to 32 percent in 2014. Traffic delays for commuters have increased by 62 percent since 1990. Automobiles and trucks stalled in traffic jams augment fuel consumption and add additional carbon to our planet's atmosphere.

Our communication equipment has fallen behind connectivity in Europe and Asia. Maintenance programs for public buildings, national forests, and national parks have been underfunded. As our infrastructure crumbles, the price of repairs continues to escalate. Delaying necessary expenditures is not cost-effective. As the old-timers used to say, "A stitch in time saves nine."

Government taxation and resource allocation should be crafted to strengthen the nation. Investing in education and infrastructure improves commerce. A quality education system increases the productivity of all young people in our society, and especially those who have special aptitudes. Modern infrastructure facilitates business activity and strengthens our economy. We should increase our investments in leading-edge educational opportunities and up-to-date transportation and communication infrastructure.

DETRIMENTAL PRIORITIES

The decision makers in Washington seem to have other priorities. There are strong incentives for our representatives to create legislation that favors corporations and wealthy individuals who are ready and willing to finance reelection campaigns. It is not by chance that lobbying in Washington has become a three-billion-dollar-a-year industry. Legislators and other government officials are accosted every day by thousands of corporate lobbyists. Rather than focusing on long-term goals that fortify our nation, legislators often construct bills with special provisions that provide immediate benefits for campaign contributors. This is not quite as bad as accepting bags full of cash from the robber barons as in the 1890s, but it is not an optimal way to manage our nation.

There is a simple explanation why our tax code is ten times as lengthy, on average, as comparable legislation in European countries. For many years, politicians in Washington have been adding special adjustments and deductions for individuals and companies as payback for reelection campaign contributions. Our representatives in Washington engage in a profitable business: tax breaks for sale. This provides special advantages for wealthy people and wealthy corporations. Wealthy individuals are often taxed at half the rate of average taxpayers.[6] Before the recent tax legislation, large multinational corporations commonly paid much lower tax rates than small businesses. This discriminated against small businesses and innovative young entrepreneurs. The playing field has been tilted in favor of established businesses that received these perks. The new tax law still provides special benefits for the largest corporations. This stifles innovation and decreases our nation's competitiveness in the global economy.

During the 1950s and 1960s, the American economy grew at a rate never seen before. The middle class expanded, home ownership increased substantially, and the country was infused with economic optimism. Interestingly enough, our tax system at that time was still based on the footing that had been necessary for fighting World War II. The tax system was highly progressive, with wealthy Americans contributing more than 50 percent of their income to the federal government. This tax arrangement may have been partially responsible for the economic success of our country during those two decades. When tax rates were subsequently reduced in the 1970s and thereafter, our economy softened, middle-class growth faltered, and the gap between rich and poor began to increase. Maybe there is a financial lesson to be learned from our history.

Previous chapters have described modifications that could reduce federal spending on health care and defense. The dollars gained by introducing a market-based universal health care system could be invested in education. Workers need extensive training to prosper in a modern global economy. Taking advantage of the potential economic contributions of all of our young people would enhance commerce and increase government income from taxation. Reducing spending on military personnel and shifting these resources to infrastructure improvements would create a large number of more productive jobs and reduce the cost of doing business in the United States.

BROAD BASE, LOW RATES

American and international economists consistently advocate a simple underlying principle for a beneficial taxation system.[7] This prescription, "broad base, low rates," recommends taxing a wide range of economic activity while keeping the rate for each tax at a low level. Most economists believe that tax policy could be arranged in such a way as to avoid distortions in business decisions. Individuals and corporations should conduct business based on market realities rather than on an attempt to game the government's taxation system. This consideration provides a clear rationale for eliminating special exemptions, deductions, credits, and allowances that favor particular business activities.

PROGRESSIVE TAXATION

Another widely accepted principle by economists is the notion that taxes should be levied in a progressive fashion.[8] Individuals who benefit the most from a robust economic system should return a larger proportion of their income to the government coffers. Those who profit from a well-organized business environment, from modern transportation and communication systems, from patent and copyright laws, and from police, fire, and disaster protection ought to be willing to contribute a significant part of their income to pay for these public investments. This is especially compelling if the tax money is invested in a manner that improves commerce. More robust economic activity augments the opportunity to make larger profits. A strong military, defending the homeland, is of much greater importance to a wealthy person than someone who is poor. It is sensible for those individuals who gain the most to consider their federal tax as a down payment on future income. A highly progressive tax system is not inconsistent with the self-interests of wealthy Americans.

Adam Smith, an early advocate of a market-based economy, encouraged progressive taxation: "It is not very unreasonable that the rich should contribute to the public expense, not only in proportion to their revenue, but something more than in proportion." [9] F. A. Hayek, a noted Austrian economist, also provided rational justification: "A person who commands more of the resources of the society will also gain proportionately more from what the government has contributed." [10] Our goal should be to extract contributions from individuals and corporations in a way that enhances business opportunities and benefits all of our citizens.

ELIMINATING EXEMPTIONS AND DEDUCTIONS

Currently, there are hundreds of deductions and other giveaways that benefit the favored few. Permitting tax deductions for some causes and not others establishes government policy for decisions that should be made by individuals. It is inappropriate to ask taxpayers to subsidize organizations whose activities offend their moral, religious, or political beliefs or their sense of fairness. Nor is government the proper agency to determine which personal expenditures should be rewarded with special tax treatment. Tax adjustments and deductions represent an implementation of the belief that people need to have a nanny government. Making this revision would be a major departure from current practice in which many taxpayers are able to take deductions for mortgage interest and for contributions to religious and charitable organizations and a myriad of other expenditures. Most economists believe that these special preferences significantly reduce government income and provide almost no benefit to our country's economy.

The complexity of our current system resides in these mysterious and impenetrable deductions and adjustments. The modifications over the past thirty-five years have come to provide copious benefits for people with large incomes. The tax system has been shaped in a manner that reflects the political power of wealthy Americans. The more a family earns, the larger the benefit of the deductions and adjustments. This is why an income of several million dollars is often taxed at a 15 percent rate while an income of forty thousand dollars is taxed at a 25 percent rate. The current arrangements continue to be the exact opposite of what is meant by progressive taxation.

The US Treasury estimates that the deductions in our tax code for individuals and corporations reduce government income by approximately $1.2 trillion each year. These tax breaks cost the government 37 percent of the tax revenue that would have otherwise been collected without them.[11] This is more than our government spends on Medicare and Medicaid. It is also more than what is distributed each year in Social Security payments.

Eliminating all tax deductions would also provide a tremendous simplification of the tax system. Our tax forms, even for individuals with limited income, have become so complicated that taxpayers need a sophisticated computer program or a professional advisor to file properly. Today barely 10 percent of Americans complete their tax returns without professional help. With no deductions, each household would report all the sources of ordinary income it received, calculate the tax, and write a check or request a refund. This would eliminate many jobs for tax professionals but would be a cause of great celebration for other Americans.

NONESSENTIAL DEDUCTIONS

We live on a planet with a population of seven billion humans. There are serious problems with pollution of the air and water, shortages of tillable land, and devastation of forests and wildlife. A visitor from another solar system might observe that our species has become a plague on our planet, upsetting the natural balance among the various life-forms that inhabit the earth. At this time in our history, maybe we should emphasize quality of child care rather than family size. A government financial incentive for having large families is unnecessary and counterproductive. Childbearing should be based on an emotional and financial commitment to provide properly for every child.

Tax deductions for dependents should be replaced with additional direct support for health care and education. It would also be helpful to provide greater federal financial assistance for K–12. These changes at the federal level would benefit parents and reduce property taxes for everyone. The nation's goal should be quality care for every child. Providing tax deductions for large families is not the optimal method to achieve this goal.

Removal of the deduction for children would be a significant change in our tax system. The impact of this alteration, however, would apply to less than half of American households. Of the households with children (38.6 percent), 40.3 percent have one child and 34.3 percent have two children. Of all households in America, only 9.7 percent have more than two children.[12]

Eliminating the deductions for mortgage payments and for charitable contributions would also dramatically change our tax system. Our current policy of excluding interest paid on mortgages would appear to be a welfare system for the wealthy. About 75 percent of this $100 billion deduction goes to taxpayers with incomes of more than $100,000 per year.[13] Eliminating this deduction is not likely to have a negative impact on home ownership. The percentage of families that own their own home in countries that have this deduction is essentially the same as in countries that do not have this deduction. In both cases, approximately 65 percent of families own homes.[14]

The deductions for charitable organizations also reduce tax payments by tens of billions of dollars.[15] The removal of this deduction by Austria, Finland, Ireland, Italy, New Zealand, Sweden, and Switzerland did not produce a significant drop in charitable contributions in these foreign countries. It appears that most people will contribute to good causes whether or not they receive a tax break.

SIMPLIFYING THE TAX CODE

Reducing the burden of complex tax forms, tax fraud, and heavy taxes on the middle class is not difficult. The obvious solution is a revised tax code that dramatically simplifies our tax forms, removes almost all income deductions, and enhances the progressiveness of the current tax brackets. The major sources of income that are currently taxed by the federal government can be divided into several distinct segments: personal income from wages and salaries, personal income from capital gains, income from the settlement of estates, and corporate income. How these sources are taxed has a profound effect on economic activity.

PERSONAL INCOME

Personal income covers wages, salary, interest, dividends, prizes, tips, and lottery winnings. Each individual would be required to report all of his or her personal income. Income from capital gains would be treated separately. Married individuals would each be taxed on one-half of their joint income. The only deductions should be contributions to retirement accounts, income received from the universal stipend (see chapter 4), state income taxes, and local property taxes. Taxation should be vigorously progressive. Anyone with annual taxable personal income greater than $10,000 should be required to file a tax form. The taxable amount earned between $10,000 and $30,000 should be taxed at 10 percent. Income from $30,000 to $80,000 should be taxed at 15 percent. Earnings between $80,000 and $125,000 should be taxed at 20 percent. Personal income between $125,000 and $250,000 should be taxed at 30 percent. Income between $250,000 and $500,000 should be taxed at 40 percent. Income greater than $500,000 should be taxed at 50 percent.

These numbers do not include each citizen's income from the universal stipend I have proposed, $9,600 per year for every citizen eighteen years of age or older. Thus, a taxable personal income of $40,000 for a married couple actually represents a disposable income of $59,200. For a single person, a taxable income of $40,000 represents a disposable income of $49,600. Individuals would also not have deductions from their paychecks for Medicare or Medicaid. My proposed universal health care plan (chapter 5) would be paid for from general tax revenues.

In examining these numbers, it is important to note that married persons would be taxed individually at these rates on one-half of their combined personal incomes. Married couples with a single earner in the family would benefit from this arrangement. Couples with one person staying home to care for children would each pay taxes on one-half of the breadwinner's income. Couples who are both working would each pay taxes on one-half of their joint income. (A projection of retirement income for a typical couple is provided in the appendix.) This assessment would seem to indicate that the financial arrangement described should provide an adequate retirement income.

This tax proposal, combined with my plans for market-based universal health care, for a universal safety net, and for mandatory employment-based contributions to a personal retirement account (2.5 percent by employer, 2.5 percent by employee), would permit the elimination of the current systems for old-age financial help (Social Security), medical reimbursements (Medicare and Medicaid), and a myriad of government programs to aid the indigent. Given that most economists have concluded that Social Security, Medicare, Medicaid, and many of our welfare programs are financially unsustainable without major increases in taxation or decreases in benefits, my proposals should be judged on their merits in comparison with the possible alternatives. In the near future, major changes will be inevitable. Confronting this challenge now may be better than waiting until our country's finances become so disastrous that nonoptimal, painful legislation is required.

The change in the personal tax rate enacted by Congress in 2018 provides a reduction in rates for most Americans but provides the largest benefits for the wealthy. The reduction in the rate for the top tier of incomes from 39.6 percent to 37 percent would seem to be unnecessary. Most wealthy individuals will benefit greatly from investment income generated by lower taxes on corporations. These tax reductions will add significantly to our country's debt. The enactment, at a time when the economy is strong, is unfortunate. Tax reductions are most sensible during recessions. When the business cycle is strong, tax collections should be used to reduce the national debt.

CAPITAL GAINS

Income from selling property would be taxed separately. It would not be reported on the annual federal income tax form. This would apply to corporations and to individuals. These transactions would include real estate, stocks, bonds, mutual funds, other financial instruments, precious metals, antiques, furniture, home decorations, and so on. The exchange of property would be taxed only if the seller made a profit. Property sold at a loss would have no tax implications. Losses from property sales would not carry over as deductions against future profits. Taxes would be paid at the time of the sale on the gain in value (the profit) and would depend on the length of ownership, as listed in figure 8.1.

Length of Ownership	Tax Rate on Gain in Value
0 to 72 hours	70%
72 hours to 30 days	50%
30 days to 1 year	25%
1 year to 10 years	15%
10 years to 20 years	10%
More than 20 years	5%

Figure 8.1: Capital Gain Tax Based on Length of Ownership

When there are multiple purchase dates on the same property, standard first-in, first-out accounting would be employed. With this system, preparing an annual federal tax return by individuals and corporations would not involve entering any information on capital gains.

There are also additional benefits of this tax arrangement. As the value of the dollar decreases over time, the property owner's "profit" reflects the effect of inflation in addition to the actual increase in the real value of the property. The lower tax rate on property held for many years mitigates the effect of inflation.

Amplifying the impact of length of ownership on the capital gain tax would also diminish the banking community's enthusiasm for speculative investments. Instead of creating hundreds of pages of complex regulations, a simple change in the tax system would provide effective financial disincentives. The nation's recent experience in which major banks participated in Wild West financial transactions resulted in a recession that caused major losses for millions of middle-class people. This, all by itself, should be sufficient justification for implementing this novel approach.

Current market activity based on flash trading does very little to benefit the general economy and hurts the long-term investor. Successful flash traders reduce the earnings of individuals who are putting money aside for their retirement years. High-frequency trading of stocks and bonds currently accounts for as much as 50 percent of the volume on American exchanges. In 1940, newly purchased stocks were held, on average, about seven years. The average duration of ownership in 1987 was only two years. In more recent times (2007), the average length of ownership was seven months. Investors that purchase stock with the intention of accumulating funds for their retirement years receive a reduction in their eventual earnings as flash traders repeatedly extract a portion of the returns that would otherwise accrue. A small tax, possibly less than one-quarter of 1 percent of the trade value, would produce a significant increment in government funding and could dampen the frequency of these flash trades. This would benefit long-term investors without setting hard-and-fast rules that can be inappropriate in some market situations.

A tax based on length of ownership would also apply to CEOs' manipulation of their companies' stock price with a company buyback to fatten their own paychecks. Our economy would be greatly improved if management decisions were based on long-term business considerations rather than on chicanery that augments CEO compensation.

SETTLING ESTATES

Theodore Roosevelt thought that passing fortunes from one generation to the next was "of great and genuine detriment to the community at large."[16] Andrew Carnegie argued that the "parent who leaves his son enormous wealth generally deadens the talents and energies of the son and tempts him to lead a less useful and less worthy life."[17]

The current estate tax affects only a few citizens. Approximately 2.5 million Americans die each year. The estate tax currently applies only to families with a net worth greater than $10.9 million. Approximately five thousand estates pay an estate tax each year. A bit of math indicates that only one out of every five hundred estates pay an estate tax.[18] This tax is a minor source of income for our government and with the 2018 changes passed by Congress that raise the threshold, this tax will become even less productive of tax revenue. Even so, many federal legislators repeatedly call for a repeal of this tax, apparently because they think it is too much of a burden on American multimillionaires. A policy that promotes a hereditary elite creates a society that is economically unhealthy and politically unfair.

My proposal for setting estates is innovative and economically beneficial. If the deceased designates the entire estate to his or her spouse, there would be no tax consequence. The deceased would also have had the option of leaving a portion of the estate to a living spouse, free of any tax, and distributing the remaining part to other people or to corporate organizations. Distributions to other living people, up to one million dollars for each person, would have no tax consequence for the recipients or the estate. The estate would pay a tax of 40 percent at the time of transfer on the amount beyond one million dollars designated for a single living person. There would be no tax consequence for the recipient. Funds designated in the deceased's will for recipients under the age of eighteen could be managed by a financial guardian until the recipient became of age.

All money designated for nonhuman recipients would be taxed at 40 percent at the time of transfer. This would include donations to corporations, partnerships, charitable organizations, and religious organizations.

If the deceased had no spouse, and if the estate distributed $10 million to ten or more human recipients, each receiving $1 million or less, there would be no tax consequences for the estate or the recipients. If the $10 million estate were distributed equally to two children and three grandchildren, each person would receive $1.6 million and the government would receive $2 million in taxes. If the deceased designated half of this estate to a spouse and half to one child, the spouse would receive $5 million tax-free, the child would receive $3 million, and the government would receive $2 million in taxes.

If the estate were worth $100 million, a spouse could receive $50 million tax-free and fifty other living recipients could each receive $1 million tax-free. The government would receive nothing at the time of transfer, and the recipients would not be taxed on the money they received.

An estate of $3 million or $4 million could easily be allocated in a manner that produced no tax consequences for either the estate or the recipients. Estates of lesser values, the most common situation, would face no tax issues in their distribution.

The objective of these tax provisions is to encourage wealthy persons to distribute their estates to people rather than organizations and to spread the money among multiple recipients. This arrangement should stimulate the general economy by increasing the number of recipients who are likely to reintroduce the money into the general economy. Less-wealthy recipients tend to spend newly acquired funds more rapidly than wealthy individuals. Spreading the estates of highly successful people to a wider range of beneficiaries might enhance commerce since more individuals would have funds for starting a new business, which is the major source of new jobs.

CORPORATE TAXES

It is reasonable to ask corporations to contribute their fair share of tax revenue. Both large and small businesses profit from public educational systems, transportation infrastructure, law enforcement, and fire protection. Federal welfare programs enhance business opportunities by increasing the number of potential customers. Government expenditures made possible by tax revenues augment economic activity. What goes around comes around.

The idea of a level playing field can be applied to American businesses as well as individuals. Our American corporate tax system has been more onerous than taxes in other nations. The nominal tax rate prior to 2019 for American companies was 35 percent. This compares with tax rates on other democratic nations that average around 20 percent. Most of the large American companies, however, have not been paying 35 percent of their profits to Uncle Sam. They have received copious adjustments, deductions, and other tax preferences. In the years 2008–2010, large US companies paid an average federal tax of 12.6 percent of their profits.[19]

The current corporate tax system penalizes small companies that do not have a large contingent of lobbyists to garner special tax advantages or a big legal department to create shadow companies overseas to reduce taxation. Small businesses without these advantages are currently taxed at the new corporate rate of 21 percent on their profits. This percentage hinders our economy. Small businesses create many more jobs in this country than the large international corporations. Correcting this inequity will create additional employment opportunities and augment our national economy.

My proposal is to base corporate taxes on a simple tally of income minus expenses. The advantages would be a level playing field for all companies, a major reduction in complexity, a reduction in the incentive for companies to lobby for tax breaks, and a significant barrier to tax cheating. Replacing the employer's requirement to pay a portion of each employee's Social Security and Medicare taxes with a 2.5 percent contribution to each employee's personal retirement account would make American companies more competitive in global markets. My proposal for removing corporate health care contributions would have the same effect. European and Japanese companies do not have this expense.

As with personal taxes, most deductions should be eliminated. Negative-profit years should have no income tax consequences. Companies would pay federal taxes only in years when revenue minus expenses is positive. The 2018 tax bill that reduced the base rate from 35 percent to 21 percent is a step in the right direction. Eliminating more deductions and having all companies—large and small—pay a base rate of 15 percent would be desirable.

Acquisition of office and production equipment, supplies, and other business resources should be expensed in the year of purchase. Business equipment, supplies, and materials would therefore be depreciated immediately. Long-term real estate acquisitions would be treated as capital investments and subject to capital gains taxation if and when they are sold. This tax liability would mirror the capital gains protocol for individuals. Real estate assets acquired as long-term investments could be "rented" by the company for their own use at market rates in a paper transaction as an annual expense to influence profitability calculations. When these assets are sold, however, the value of each asset for capital gains treatment would be calculated as the selling price plus the cumulative rental income minus the purchase price. If this value is negative, there would be no tax consequence. Investments by financial institutions in instruments, such as real estate, stocks, or bonds, would be subject to the same capital gains protocol as described for personal income.

The United States is unusual in that it does not tax corporate income that is earned outside the country until these funds are brought home. Parking their earnings in foreign countries has permitted a number of large corporations to reduce their tax payments. Earnings in foreign countries should be taxed in the same way as domestic earnings, with the exception that taxes paid to foreign countries would be deductible from the corporate income tax.

A curiosity of the American tax system is the absence of a value-added tax (VAT).[20] This tax is employed by 175 countries. The United States is the only rich country that has not implemented the VAT. This is a bit strange because this tax is easy to collect and difficult to avoid. The computation of this tax appears to be somewhat complex, but in reality it is quite simple. The required information is routinely collected by every company and the math is trivial for modern computers.

The VAT most governments collect is computed by adding up the value of the service provided by each participant involved in the production and sale of a product, from raw materials to the ultimate purchase by the consumer. Each company along the chain pays a tax on the value it added to the product. The tax payment is a percentage of the value added by each contributor to the product's ultimate retail price.

The VAT system reduces tax collection problems. A major advantage is that the tax is invisible to the consumer. Unlike the traditional sales tax, no extra charge is added at the point of sale. Because each participant along the production, distribution, and sale of the product reports the information required to compute the tax, cheating is difficult. Any participant who fails to report accurately will contravene data from his supplier or buyer. The VAT is generally independent of local sales taxes.

Salaries and wages are not included in the computation. Nor are the costs of office space, office supplies, production equipment, and legal resources included. The tax would be based only on the difference between the selling price and the price of the materials purchased. If the percentage paid to the IRS were something like 10 percent, this tax would produce an amount of income for the government that would be substantial. The VAT would be an addition to the corporate income tax.

TAXES ON UNDESIRABLE BEHAVIOR

Governments can use tax policy to discourage behavior that erodes the common good. Many things that people do are harmful to their local community and to the country as a whole. Placing a cost on those behaviors might decrease their frequency. In a free society, this policy is preferred to simply outlawing these actions. The funds collected from these sin taxes can be employed to counter some of the negative impacts that these undesirable behaviors produce.[21]

An early case of this type of tax is one on gasoline and diesel fuel. With millions of automobiles and trucks in our country, major investments are required to construct roads, bridges, and traffic-control equipment. The primary financial burden falls on our government. Since some individuals drive vehicles much more often than others, it makes sense to collect taxes from those who travel frequently. Taxing gasoline and diesel fuel accomplishes this goal. Motor vehicles that are powered by fossil fuels have major health ramifications. Their engine exhaust degrades the air we breathe, creating serious health problems. Taxing motor fuels can also provide funds to cover the medical expenses that are needed to treat pulmonary and cardiac damage.

Federal and state taxes on gasoline in the United States average fifty-three cents per gallon. In Western Europe, the average tax on gasoline is slightly more than three dollars a gallon. Compared to drivers in other countries, Americans are very lightly taxed.[22] Given the costly impact of maintaining our transportation system, it would be very sensible for our state and federal legislators to increase the current fuel tax.

Many Americans continue to smoke cigarettes. This habit has been shown to have significant negative health impacts. Given the cost of maintaining our public health care system, all of us should be happy if tobacco addicts were required to cover a heftier portion of the cost of their behavior. It is bad enough for smokers to engage in behavior that compromises their own health. Expecting nonsmokers to cover the cost of the damage is unreasonable. Taxing tobacco is an extremely rational policy. Europeans have recognized this reality. Cigarettes in the United States are taxed at an average of $3 per pack. In Europe, the average is around $6 per pack. Our tax on tobacco should be increased.[23]

In recent years, several states have legalized the recreational use of marijuana. The health effects of this new legislation are unclear. Taxing the sale of marijuana will provide funding to study the effects of this change and to cover medical costs that may result from this experiment.

America, like many other countries, has been experiencing an epidemic of obesity. This has greatly increased health care expenses for the nation. The added cost of treating the multitude of health problems that arise from obesity adds an unnecessary burden on Medicare and Medicaid. Taxing eating habits that contribute to obesity would be a sensible government policy. Several countries have recently introduced a tax on foods and drinks that are heavily laden with sugar. This tax applies to purchases of products such as carbonated drinks and candy bars.[24] The additional funds provided by this tax would help cover the public expense of the medical consequences of obesity and might lower the consumption of unwholesome foods.[25]

Beginning in the 1990s, there has been a noticeable increase in the frequency of extreme weather events and a small increase in the average global temperatures. Scientists believe that the high level of CO_2 and methane emissions are responsible for these changes. There is an international consensus that the generation of these two gases by industrial companies and transportation vehicles should be reduced. In the absence of coordinated action, the continued warming of the atmosphere is expected to melt the polar ice caps, raise sea levels, and inundate many of the world's coastal cities. Consequently, countries around the globe are implementing or considering implementing a tax on carbon emissions to restrain the production of CO_2 and methane. The money generated by this tax could be used for coastal infrastructure improvements to combat the rising sea levels. In addition, this tax will encourage companies and individuals to develop new technologies that fulfill our energy needs without producing CO_2 and methane. This carbon tax could have a beneficial impact for all of us.

———

My taxation proposals strive to simplify the process and provide a structure in which those who are economically successful contribute more proportionately than people who are not so fortunate. Economies are more productive when all citizens do well. When a nation's wealth is concentrated among a small elite, economic growth slows, and recessions are more likely. Closing the gap between the 99 percent and the 1 percent improves spending and augments commerce. This will reduce social unrest, increase confidence in our governmental processes, enhance business opportunities, grow the middle class, and amplify corporate profitability. A healthy economy is especially beneficial for those who are wealthy. Is it not fair and reasonable to ask those who benefit the most from constructive government investments to be taxed on a greater percentage of their incomes?

The economist Thomas Piketty provides a compact economic model that is based on the observation that the rate of return on capital has historically been greater than the general growth rate of the economy as a whole.[26] Faster growth in wealth than in GDP means a steady increase in inequality. Those who are born rich have an advantage financially over those who start with minimal capital. Working hard and making intelligent business decisions have a much greater probability of success if one starts with ample financial resources. A more progressive system in which wealthy individuals pay a higher percentage of their income in taxes will strengthen our economy by providing financial support for improved education and modernization of our infrastructure. Improving the opportunity for more individuals to engage successfully in the nation's commerce will benefit all of us.

Lowering corporate tax rates might have a less negative effect on federal income than one might first think. Lowering tax rates on corporations should increase company profits, empower business investment, create more jobs, and increase dividends to shareholders. With a stronger economy, the lower tax rate would be applied to a larger base income. In addition, more profitable companies would be distributing more dividends to shareholders. These individuals would pay additional personal taxes on their increased incomes.

REDUCING APRIL 15 INDIGESTION

Simplification of the tax system has obvious benefits.[27] If the IRS received data from employers on payments to their employees along with data on purchases and income from sales, and investment companies also reported relevant data on income received by their customers, IRS computers could prefill all of the fields on the standard 1040 tax form.[28] The taxpayer would review the form and sign it if the entries were accurate. Only when a discrepancy was detected would there be effort required by the taxpayer. In those cases, the individual would contact the IRS to make corrections. This would save an enormous amount of time for taxpayers and reduce administrative costs for the IRS.[29]

It is difficult to estimate how much tax income my proposals would generate. Trickle-down economics has failed to boost our economy and therefore has not increased tax collections. My proposal to reduce federal health care and defense expenditures would enable additional funding for education and infrastructure improvements. Both of these investments would improve the economy and thus produce additional tax revenues. Making the tax schedule for personal income more progressive would have the same effect. My proposal for taxing property sales at the time of exchange as a replacement for the current capital gains system might also augment our government's income.

Whether these changes would balance federal expenditures with federal income is difficult to predict. However, these proposals for spending and taxation can be implemented with numbers that eventually produce a balanced budget. It is likely that the various components will need to be recurrently adjusted until the desired outcome is obtained. Why not replace the current system that regularly generates unsustainable deficits with one that has a reasonable chance of producing a balanced budget?

Chapter 9

GOVERNMENT REGULATIONS

Let America realize that self-scrutiny is not treason.
Self-examination is not disloyalty.
— CARDINAL RICHARD CUSHING

Joseph Stiglitz, a Nobel Prize–winning economist, in his 2016 book, *Rewriting the Rules of the American Economy*, offers an assessment of our predicament. His perspective is summarized on the book's cover: "The United States bills itself as the land of opportunity, a place where anyone can achieve success and a better life through hard work and determination. But the facts tell a different story—the U. S. today lags behind most other developed nations in measures of inequality and economic mobility. For decades, wages have stagnated for the majority of workers while economic gains have disproportionately gone to the top one percent. Education, housing and healthcare—essential ingredients for individual success—are growing ever more expensive. American inequality is the result of misguided structural rules that actually constrict economic growth. We have stripped away worker protections and family support systems, created a tax system that rewards short-term gains over long-term investment, offered a de facto public safety net to too-big-to-fail financial institutions, and chosen monetary and fiscal policies that promote wealth over full employment."[1]

During the twentieth century, political movements in Russia and China attempted to create governments that could meet the needs of the common people. These efforts provided empirical evidence that top-down control of a complex economy often leads to despotic rule. The theories of Marx and Lenin have failed to deliver the goods and services that most people desire. Instead, communism has diminished personal freedom. It has been a disastrous experiment.

A bottom-up process in which companies compete for consumers has proved to be more successful. Unfortunately, recent history has also demonstrated that market economies can produce undesirable outcomes. Individuals who are poor, unhealthy, or aged often struggle to keep afloat. Children who lack health care, quality education, and job opportunities face a formidable challenge. For several decades, the nation's GDP has expanded but the benefits have gone to a limited number of very wealthy people.

Market forces often beget results in which a few people acquire considerable wealth while others are left behind. Outcomes are shaped by the statutes that regulate commerce. Lobbyists have biased the wording of legislation in ways that make our economy less efficient and less fair for small-business owners. Legislators should align tax policy with incentives that stimulate competition and foster positive social returns. Although corporate lobbying can provide our representatives in Washington with useful information that often improves legislation, it has also frequently engendered laws that harm workers, subsidize non-productive business practices, and allow corporations to avoid responsibility for environmental damage. Changing the rules of our market economy to foster equal opportunity for all of our citizens will stabilize the business environment and bring prosperity to more people.

Regulations to ensure competitiveness were passed in the age of the robber barons to control the excesses of monopolistic practices and the formation of trusts that could dictate prices. The Interstate Commerce Commission was created in 1887 and the Sherman Antitrust Act was enacted in 1890. Early in the 1900s, the Federal Trade Commission was formed and the Clayton Act passed. These legislative acts were effective in increasing competition in the marketplace and stimulating economic activity.

In the 1970s, Congress developed a fever for deregulation. Key industries, including trucking, natural gas, railroads, telecommunications, and airlines, were deregulated. These changes erased the beneficial effect of the earlier legislation. Corporate giants began to dominate markets by stifling competition. Monopolistic control permitted major players to dictate prices and control product quality.[2] Today, dominant firms receive sheltered regulatory treatment. Large American corporations collectively invest $3 billion a year to influence legislators. Crony capitalism misshapes what would otherwise be a competitive market.[3]

RESTRICTING COMPETITION

It is time to examine the role of dominant players in industries that have little competition from foreign companies, such as the pharmaceutical industry, airlines, telecommunications, and internet-service provision. In many of these industries, prices are 50 percent higher than in other wealthy countries. The robber baron quandary of the 1890s has returned with a vengeance. Federal regulation is needed to prevent tyranny by corporate giants. Legislation that breaks up noncompetitive industries will engender quality service and fair pricing.

Well-established companies with significant market share have also increasingly engaged in buyouts of innovative small firms that have the potential to offer competition. These acquisitions derail the possibility that powerful incumbents might be replaced by young upstarts with superior technology. Consumers are the losers since these business deals remove the incentive for major corporations to improve products and reduce prices. Federal regulators should take action to discourage this distortion of an otherwise healthy marketplace.

Our economy could also be enhanced by refining our immigration priorities. Increasing the relative emphasis on admission of immigrants that add technological skills and other abilities that promote successful business activity would be helpful.

Government practices that promote noncompetitive bidding also compromise the efficiency of our market system. Sole-source contracting in the defense industry increases costs and reduces military readiness. Government contracts should be open to competitive bidding with decisions based on price and quality rather than on the size of corporate donations to political campaigns.

Laws that restrict government agencies from negotiating volume pricing for goods and services also impede the market. When Congress extended Medicare to cover the cost of prescription drugs, the legislation specifically prevented Medicare from using its purchasing power to reduce costs.[4] The Veterans Administration currently negotiates the price of prescription drugs for veterans. Taxpayers would save hundreds of millions of dollars if Medicare and Medicaid had similar options.

The US Patent and Trademark Office has also limited competition and inhibited creativity. Patents are supposed to encourage the development of cutting-edge technologies by providing a period of several years when inventors have the exclusive right to market their inventions. The Patent Office for decades, however, has issued patents that give companies monopolies on products that are minor variants of existing merchandise or minor changes to established methodologies. Companies that receive copycat patents improve their profits but do not provide a meaningful contribution to the nation's technology.

The Patent Office has been especially egregious in approving patents for pharmaceuticals that mimic existing products. The negative effect of this practice is augmented by our government's placement of a prescription requirement on many drugs that are sold over the counter in other countries. The United States is one of the few countries that allow direct advertising of prescription drugs. One would think that a drug that can be taken only when prescribed by a medical doctor is too dangerous to be advertised to the general public. There is also another inappropriate practice. Unlike in most nations, pharmaceutical companies in the United States are permitted to offer inducements to medical professionals to prescribe their products. It is not a surprise that Americans pay substantially more for drugs than the citizens of other countries.

During the 1990s, when my company was building fraud-detection models for major banks, a competing firm applied for a patent for using a computer to detect credit card fraud. Supposedly, patents are not supposed to be granted when there is "prior art." In this case, computers had already been used for fraud detection for over five years by several major credit card issuers. The company's lawyer also requested a patent for using a well-known computer technique to analyze credit card fraud. Patents were granted for both claims. The employees at the Patent Office apparently had failed to do their homework.

The Patent Office's penchant for issuing patents for trivial innovations should be stopped. Congress might pass a law limiting the number of patents (say one hundred per year) that can be issued. Only novel inventions deserve patents. Patents should be neither a barrier to innovation nor a pathway to unnecessary litigation.

The United States currently has some of the highest prices in the world for internet service. In addition, our service is not among the leaders in terms of speed. How is it that the country that invented the internet is neither a price leader nor a speed leader?[5] Companies with well-financed lobbyists and an appetite for acquiring competitors have gained control of the market. Today's robber barons dominate telecommunications and software platforms rather than railroads. Legislators, with campaign contributions in their pockets, have even approved laws in twenty states that prohibit cities from laying fiber-optic cables.

Without competition, there is no incentive for a dominant company to improve service. Clearly, as in the 1890s, legislation is required to provide an open, fair market that permits small businesses to compete with the modern giants of industry. Our economy would greatly benefit from a level playing field.

Laws meant to eliminate unfair corporate actions are ineffective when the government has insufficient funds to enforce the laws. Action by legislators to underfund regulatory agencies is commonly encouraged by lobbyists. A good example is funding provided for the IRS. Between 2010 and 2014, budget limitations required the IRS to make a 10 percent reduction in staff.[6] An analysis of IRS performance suggests that every dollar spent on investigating suspicious tax returns produces $200 in additional taxes. The same congressmen who decry deficit spending pass budget constraints that significantly reduce the nation's tax income.

RISKY BANKING

Our country's financial system has gradually evolved in a way that tilts the playing field to benefit big banks. Toward the end of the last century, the financial sector was deregulated. Banks were permitted to combine traditional banking with speculative investing. Large banks, because they play a crucial role in the nation's economy, have become "too big to fail." If these banks were to go under, the entire economy of our country would be in serious trouble. Bankers, with this knowledge, have taken substantial risks knowing deals that went south would receive a federal bailout. When the risky bets are profitable, money pours into the bankers' pockets. When the bets fail, however, taxpayers are left with the bill. Heads, the banks win; tails, the taxpayers lose. Is it any surprise that the big banks recently managed to precipitate the worst economic recession our country has suffered since the 1929 debacle?

The absence of sensible regulations cost millions of Americans their homes and their lifetime savings. It is a national disgrace that the individuals who destroyed our economy paid themselves large bonuses with government bailout money. In addition, very few of the people who engaged in excessive risks lost their jobs or were fined for failure to meet their fiduciary responsibilities. Our representatives in Washington need to listen less intently to the lobbyists and be more concerned with their responsibilities to all American citizens.

Given the cost of running a political campaign, candidates often believe there is no way to win without accepting funds from corporations and wealthy Americans. Most citizens are unaware that lobbying public officials was not always the norm. In 1874 the US Supreme Court, in *Trist v. Child*, ruled that lobbying was inconsistent with our constitution and laws. The Court defended this decision in simple language: "If any of the great corporations of the country were to hire adventurers who make market of themselves . . . to procure passage of a general law with a view to promotion of their private interests, the moral sense of every right-minded man would instinctively denounce the employer and employed as steeped in corruption, and the employment as infamous."

It is unclear why our courts over the past 140 years have come to accept political bribery.[7] What was true in 1874 is still true today. The Supreme Court's recent decision to grant unlimited political spending by corporations and wealthy individuals in order to protect freedom of speech is arbitrary and unreasonable. This principle becomes a charade when the wealthy and powerful provide funds that allow one candidate to dominate radio, TV, and print media. In addition, politicians and government employees should be prohibited from working for companies doing business with the government for at least five years after they leave office or federal employment. Isn't it time to make a serious effort to eliminate the political corruption that currently dominates Washington politics?[8]

What is needed is legislation that, once again, limits the influence corporate America has on our political process. A modern version of the Tillman Act that can survive scrutiny by our Supreme Court is desperately needed. Action is required to restrain present-day robber barons. This will be an uphill battle because most of our elected representatives currently receive campaign funding from the guilty parties.

Chapter 10

REJECTING PARTISAN TRIBALISM

Political parties exist to secure responsible government. . . .
Instead of instruments to promote general welfare,
they have become the tools of corrupt interests which
use them impartially to serve their selfish purposes.
—PROGRESSIVE PARTY PLATFORM OF 1912

The dysfunction that has characterized our federal government in recent years is the joint product of structural flaws in our Constitution and the rise of political parties that have come to play a dominant role in governmental processes. Party leaders orchestrate the redistricting process for the House, determine who is appointed to important legislative committees, influence who receives money for reelection campaigns, and control which legislative proposals will make it out of committee. Within this framework, our representatives are more concerned with party priorities than with solving our nation's problems.

Washington is a battleground for two private clubs aspiring to gain ascendency by controlling the White House and Congress. The bitter partisanship observed on a day-to-day basis is a direct result of this conflict. Our representatives focus on political strategies for garnering votes in the next election. They engage in political theater, depicting themselves as the good guys and the members of the other party as the bad guys. It is not a surprise that party membership among the general public appears to have been falling for several decades.[1]

A Gallup poll in December 2017 asked registered voters if they considered themselves to be Republicans, Democrats, or leaning toward one of the parties.[2] The individuals in their sample identified their preferences as 37 percent Republican and 44 percent Democratic. It is unclear whether the voters who did not indicate a preference had no opinion or just had a desire to avoid disagreeable discussions given the current contentious political environment.

The population of our country is an order of magnitude greater than during the early years of the nation. An unfortunate result of this change is that candidates for office have difficulty communicating in person with the people they wish to represent. Today it takes a considerable amount of money to campaign effectively for national office. To be successful, potential candidates need financial sponsors. One consequence is that politicians often become beholden to the individuals and companies that pay for their campaigns. Our legislators face a difficult dilemma: Should they vote for a bill they believe is best for the nation or should they cast their vote in a way that gains financial support from potential backers? The necessity of covering the cost of a future reelection campaign can heavily influence how they vote.

There does not seem to be a simple way to address this problem, especially given the recent Supreme Court decision regarding the Citizens United case.[3] Members of the House of Representatives face a campaign for reelection every two years. The day after they win it becomes necessary for them to start thinking about how to acquire financial support for the next election cycle. It might be beneficial to rethink the current arrangement in which our representatives in the House have to mount a reelection campaign every two years. Maybe four-year terms for legislators in the House might be a welcome change. This alteration would reduce the pressure on members of the House to be constantly raising campaign money. Having one's representative focus on legislative activities rather than allocating time for wooing financial supporters would be far more constructive for the general public. This might also reduce the influence of corporate lobbyists.

Another potential change would be to introduce term limits for legislators. Presidents are limited to two terms. Limiting members of the Senate and House to twelve years of service could reduce the negative impact of repeatedly running for reelection. A person reelected to a second term in the Senate could cast votes for six years based on his or her judgment on what is best for the country rather than what impact his or her vote would have on future campaign contributors. A person reelected to a third term in the House (assuming the enactment of four-year terms) would have four years to cast votes without worrying about the next reelection campaign.

My proposals in chapter 3 to alter the way we elect presidents, organize the Senate, and redistrict the House would lessen the power of the political parties. Additional changes are required, however, for voters to regain a reasonable degree of control. Extensive overhauls of the voting systems that are employed to elect our representatives at the city, state, and federal levels are needed. These procedures can be simplified and made more democratic. The objective is to separate the election process from the process of governing. There is no rational justification for having politicians and political parties control elections. As in any other important contest, the rules for voting and for counting the votes should be done by a neutral third party. We need the equivalent of professionals in striped shirts to ensure that every citizen's vote influences the outcome.

Primaries orchestrated and conducted by the two major political parties should be replaced by a single primary open to all citizens who seek public office. Each city, county, and state should be required to honor qualifications for eligibility that are consistent with our constitution and federal laws. A mechanism is needed to limit the number of candidates for any given office to a manageable number. This can be done by requiring written endorsements (i.e., signatures) from registered voters or by another means that is fair for all prospective candidates.

AN IMPROVED VOTING SYSTEM

We need a voting process that is different from the current practice. There is an innovative procedure for measuring voter preferences. Approval Voting[4] is a method that is simple to understand and one that can be implemented without difficulty. When there are more than two candidates, voters are permitted to express their support for more than one person. The voter is given a list of the people who have qualified to be a candidate. The voter checks the names of those who meet with his or her approval. Approval, in this context, means someone whom the voter believes would be capable of performing the duties of the public office in a satisfactory manner.

If there are five candidates, the voter can approve one, two, three, or even four candidates. Approving all five would, in essence, remove the voter's influence on which person might win. The result of the primary election would be to identify the two candidates who received the largest number of approval votes. These two individuals would progress to the general election, and the one receiving the most votes in that election would become the winner.

There are many advantages of this procedure compared to the current voting process. A major difference is that candidates do not have to be members of a political party. Political parties could endorse contenders and finance their campaigns. In contrast to current elections, however, the individuals selected by the two major political parties are not guaranteed a place on the general election ballot.

Voters in this type of primary system will have more impact on which person becomes the eventual winner. Seventeen candidates sought the office of president in the 2016 Republican primary. Voters were allowed to select only one of the contestants. Often this single-vote procedure favors persons on the political extreme. Voters who prefer moderates might be forced to pick one among several who would be acceptable to them. This splits the votes among moderate candidates so that none of them performs as well as they would in a two-person race. With Approval Voting, moderate candidates are not at a disadvantage. They can be endorsed by voters who also support other candidates. Each voter has the option of affirming all candidates that meet with his or her approval.

Approval Voting also encourages the voter to evaluate all candidates. Because the voter has the option of approving more than one candidate, there is an incentive to gather more information about all candidates. This would not only produce more informed voting but would also enhance public interest in the primary and increase voter turnout.

A fourth consideration is that voters would be challenged to make strategic considerations as to how many votes to cast. The advantages and disadvantages of various voting strategies would likely be discussed with friends and neighbors. These discussions would energize more people to become involved in the election process. Democracy works best when people are motivated to participate actively.

In the general election, voters would choose between the two candidates who had been endorsed by the greatest number of people. Both contestants could be from the same political party, from different parties, or from no party. This would encourage political parties to select candidates who appeal to the general populace rather than to a small group of party activists, a highly desirable change.

The states of Washington and California have recently adopted a procedure in which there is a single primary open to all individuals who wish to be candidates. These elections are not organized and administered by the two major political parties. One of the difficulties of this procedure is that one party might have five candidates for the office while the other party might have only two candidates. Because

Democrats would be spreading their votes among five candidates, even in a heavily Democratic state such as California, a nonpartisan primary could select two Republican candidates for the main election. I believe the adoption of Approval Voting in the primaries in Washington and California would eliminate the possibility that two candidates with minority support would face off in the general election. The winner of the election should be the candidate that is approved by a majority of the voters. Approval voting in a nonpartisan primary would empower voters to select the two individuals who clearly have the most overall support.

CAMPAIGN FINANCE

Another issue, campaign finance, also influences whom we elect. In our modern society, free speech is much more than the right to express opinions openly to friends, neighbors, colleagues, and local governing bodies. To effectively influence state and national elections, a candidate must have access to modern communications. Money is required to take advantage of these options. The internet, to some extent, can provide a free approach to a portion of the electorate, but traditional media (newsprint, radio, and television) comes at a cost. In urban areas, the price of access can be substantial. For many who wish to communicate their ideas and plans to voters, this expense may be prohibitive. Pay-to-play should not be a necessary requirement for citizens to seek public office.

Other nations arrange public debates to provide opportunities for candidates to make their case to the voters. My proposal for a primary process that reduces the contest to two candidates for the general election would seem to be a perfect arrangement for public financing of three or four debates prior to the general election. The format for the debates should be determined by a neutral campaign commission without interference from political parties, candidates, or lobbyists. Reasonable choices for this commission could be established journalists selected in a way that provides balance to the questions.

The format for these debates should constrain each candidate in a way that provides equal time for both speakers. A standard protocol could be implemented. At the beginning of the session, equal time allotments would be specified for both speakers. Each candidate's microphone would be active only when the moderator recognized the speaker. The length of his or her comments would be timed. Each person would have the option of allocating part of his or her time to topics unrelated to the moderator's question. When a candidate's time limit was exhausted, his or her microphone would be permanently deactivated. Since this regulatory protocol would consist entirely of switching microphones off and on and keeping track of time, the process could be assigned to a computer.

Campaign contributions for both the primary and the general election should be restricted to a maximum dollar amount from each contributor for each political office. Why is a restriction on campaign contribution a violation of free speech if all registered voters are held to the same limit? The general principle of one-person, one-vote rather than one-dollar, one-vote should hold for speech as well as the act of voting. There should be no right to drown out the opinions of others by commandeering the stage. The concept of free speech should apply to everyone, not just the wealthy. Limiting the amount of money that can be contributed by one person is a sensible way to provide a level playing field.

Corporations, unions, and foreigners should not fund political advertising nor contribute directly to campaigns. In our modern environment in which communication with other voters requires access to media outlets, free speech can be a zero-sum game. The high cost of print and electronic media messaging permits wealthy organizations to monopolize the conversation. Corporate managers and union leaders should have the same speech rights as other citizens. It is inappropriate, however, for them to use organizational funds to dominate radio and TV broadcasts. Prohibiting corporations and unions from financing political activity does not violate the principle of free speech. The logic behind the Tillman Act is more valid today than it was in 1907.

President Theodore Roosevelt, in his annual message to Congress in 1905, had something to say about corporate involvement in the election process: "All contributions by corporations to any political committee should be forbidden by law; directors should not be permitted to use stockholders' money for such purposes; and, moreover, a prohibition of this kind would be, as far as it went, an effective method of stopping the evils aimed in corrupt practices acts."[5] As noted previously, the restriction on contributions from nonhuman actors should also cover other organizations, including unions. Financing political campaigns should be limited to living, breathing registered voters.

VOTER SUPPRESSION

Our nation could also do more to prohibit voter suppression. Winning elections is the preeminent goal for both major political parties. At present, any maneuver that promotes winning is embraced. In many states, voters who support candidates of the minority party have to travel long distances to a polling site and wait hours in long lines to cast their votes. Partisan state legislators should not be setting the rules for how individuals vote in federal elections.

Recent state actions have resurrected the injustice of Jim Crow legislation that blemished our democracy in the late nineteenth century and the first half of the twentieth century. A nonpartisan commission, rather than elected officials, should make decisions regarding the number of polling places, their locations, and the number of voting machines at each location. Federal regulations should be established that bind all states to a basic set of rules for the conduct of elections for federal political offices.

A procedure that would reduce some of these inequities would be a federal mandate to register automatically every person who is authorized to receive a universal safety net stipend as proposed in chapter 4. The system for providing these stipends would be carefully regulated. This approach would enfranchise every citizen of voting age and would permit prompt removal of deceased individuals from the voting rolls. In a world of modern electronics, fraud can be easily detected if the system is operated and monitored in an intelligent fashion.

Providing an opportunity in every state for registered voters to cast their ballots by mail would remove the incentive for partisans to manipulate the number and location of polling sites. Forcing eligible individuals to jump through hoops to vote is undemocratic and unnecessary. Does anyone doubt that giving every citizen the right to vote is an essential aspect of an impartial democratic system?

Enhancing the opportunity of every citizen to participate in local, state, and federal elections should be a high priority. This requires the removal of artificial voting barriers that have been implemented for partisan advantage. It also demands rigorous restrictions on the amounts and sources of campaign funds. Adoption of Approval Voting within the context of a single nonpartisan primary would also enhance our democratic process. The individuals who are chosen to represent us in Washington and in our state capitals should be chosen by all the people in contests that are not rigged to favor special interests.

The procedures for selecting individuals to represent us in Washington should not be manipulated by state officials for partisan advantage. Would it not be reasonable to have federal voting regulations that eliminate partisan chicanery?

Chapter 11

TWO AMERICAS

What a pity beings can't exchange problems.
Everyone knows exactly how to solve the other fellow's problem.
— OLIN MILLER

The 2016 presidential election provided a powerful wake-up call for the entrenched politicians in both major political parties. Donald Trump, a businessman with no political experience, ran a successful campaign by attacking Washington politics, government policies that favored the wealthy, and foreign competition that has been destroying American jobs. He engaged in a powerful negative campaign against congressional leaders, influential CEOs, and the news media. He appealed to millions of conservative voters, including working-class whites in the Midwest, who believed Washington politicians were the enemy. Instead of attributing their problems to technological innovations and globalization, these individuals were easily convinced that the political environment in our nation's capital was the major cause of their economic distress. The desire for change, almost any change, motivated millions of Americans to vote enthusiastically for Donald Trump.

This backlash against the two major political parties should not have been unexpected. Amid growing inequality, Republicans continue to see our country as a meritocracy in which hard work and brilliance lead to well-deserved financial success. Many citizens, however, viewed this complacency as an illusion based on privilege, economic advantage, and simple self-interest. Trump contended that those with money and political clout were a self-perpetuating elite who had no concern for the misery of a large segment of the American population.

The Democratic party selected a candidate that epitomized the Washington establishment. She proposed solutions that were minor variations of existing programs. Americans are well aware that our current government's medical expenditures are unsustainable, that Social Security is also financially insecure, and that our public educational system is second-rate in a world economy that requires advanced job skills. A candidate that campaigned on "more of the same" was an unattractive option for voters desperate for change.

The mood of the country becomes apparent when one examines voting patterns across the nation. Data from the 2010 census provide information on the demographics of all 3,113 counties in the United States. Among the measures for each county are the percentage of residents who describe their race as white (% White), the percentage of residents whose educational attainment is less than a four-year college degree (% No BA), and the percentage of housing arrangements that are classified as single-family residences (% Single-Family Residences). One can calculate a composite score for each county in the United States composed of % White plus % No BA plus % Single-Family Residences. This measure has a possible range from 0 to 300. It provides a powerful indicator of how voters in each county cast their ballots in the 2016 presidential election.

These demographic characteristics, taken together, segment the voters with remarkable precision. Single-family residences predominate in rural and suburban American. Urban areas tend to have multi-family buildings. Counties that are predominately white tend to be in rural areas. Individuals with college degrees gravitate to the cities and suburbs. A composite measure that aggregates these factors captures characteristics that heavily influenced how people voted.

Figure 11.1 summarizes the relationship between this composite score for each county and the percentage of voters that cast a ballot for Donald Trump. Voting data at the state and county levels have been carefully tabulated.[1] There is a very consistent linear relationship between the composite score and the percentage of votes for Trump in each county. Counties with a score less than 140 voted primarily for Trump's opponent. On average, less than 16 percent of the votes in these counties were for Trump. In counties that had primarily white voters with no college education who lived in single-family residences (a composite score greater than 280), the vote for Trump averaged almost 80 percent. Counties in which the composite scores were intermediate between these extreme values voted, on average, in a smooth linear relationship between 16 percent and 80 percent, with lower composite scores providing fewer votes for Trump.

County Composite Score = % White + % No BA + % Single-Family Residences

Composite Score	% Vote Trump	Number of Counties	Population (Thousands)
Less Than 140	15.9	9	10,520
140 to 160	21.1	12	26,619
160 to 180	27.2	41	30,058
180 to 200	34.2	141	55,103
200 to 220	47.2	277	60,865
220 to 240	58.0	542	55,723
240 to 260	66.7	885	45,185
260 to 280	72.6	1,097	25,532
More than 280	77.9	109	1,565

Figure 11.1: Voting Preference Based on Demographic Variables

Urban voters tend to live in multiunit residences, are more likely to be nonwhite, and are more educated on average than rural voters.

In contrast, Trump's most enthusiastic supporters were primarily from small-town America where employment opportunities have been lost. Local economies on the decline have produced a shrinking tax base. Local services and public education have suffered. Falling real estate prices have attracted retirees and workers with outdated job skills. This segment of the American population was ripe for a populist candidate advocating change.

An alternate way of analyzing these relationships can be provided by presenting the voting data and census information in a different manner. Instead of organizing the information with a complex derived measure, one can directly examine the demographic characteristics of the people who voted for Trump and those who did not. Figure 11.2 orders counties by the degree of support for Trump, high to low. It then records for each group of counties the average value of three characteristics calculated by the Census Bureau. The percentage of white residents in each county is the difference between the total number of residents and those reporting to be black, Asian, Hispanic, or Native American. The percentage of residents graduating from college with a bachelor's degree is also averaged for each voting group. The third measure is the average number of persons per square mile for the counties in each grouping.

Trump Share of Votes	Number of Counties	Percent White	Percent BA Grad	Persons Per Sq. Mile
90% or more	70	87.0	18.0	15.0
80% to 90%	577	87.2	15.1	32.2
70% to 80%	927	84.5	16.0	71.0
60% to 70%	656	80.7	19.2	122.7
50% to 60%	399	72.0	21.6	226.1
40% to 50%	236	65.1	26.0	460.3
30% to 40%	147	51.1	26.9	821.9
20% to 30%	67	42.3	29.0	1,169.7
Less than 20%	33	37.4	34.2	7,567.0

Figure 11.2: Votes for Trump by Race, Education, and Population Density

There are very clear relationships between voting preferences and county demographic characteristics. Counties in which voters had an overwhelming preference (more than 90 percent) for Donald Trump were from rural areas (fifteen persons per square mile) and were predominately white (87 percent). The inverse relationship between voting for Trump and population density is remarkable. Data analysts seldom see relationships as clean and strong as this one. The data also indicated that individuals who live in counties where there are few nonwhite neighbors tend to vote for Trump. Counties that strongly supported Trump's opponent had a higher proportion of residents who had earned a college BA. For example, the counties that most strongly supported Clinton averaged 37 percent BAs. The counties that most strongly supported Trump ranged from 15 to 18 percent residents who have attained a college BA.

It is also noteworthy that in a 2016 Yale University survey, counties in which a majority of residents believed that global warming is mostly caused by human activities tended to vote for Clinton.[2] Counties in which a majority did not believe that humans are responsible for global warming tended to vote for Trump. One of the authors commented, "86% of the variation across counties in respondent's belief that 'global warming is mostly caused by human activity' is explained by voting preference."

A third demographic analysis based on summary data for all fifty states from the 2010 census provides additional information on the outcome of the 2016 presidential election. Another composite measure was computed for each of the fifty states. This measure was the percentage of citizens in each state that owned a gun (% Gun Owners) added to the percentage of adult residents whose educational attainment was less than a bachelor's degree (% No BA). The potential range for this measure is 0 to 200. The fifty states were ordered (sorted) from the highest value (Arkansas) on this composite measure to the lowest value (Rhode Island) and then placed in five groupings based on this ordering. For each state, the percentage difference in votes for Trump and Clinton was calculated and averaged for each group (Avg % Trump Advantage). The total population for each of the five groups was also recorded along with the Average GDP for the states in each group. These data are presented in figure 11.3.

State Composite Measure = % Gun Owners + % No BA

States	Avg Composite Score	Avg % Trump Advantage	Total Population (Millions)	Avg GDP Dollars (Billions)
AR WV AK ID WY AL NM MT MS LA	129.3	+25.8	23.3	86.1
KY ND SC TN NV HI IN TX IA SD	114.8	+14.7	57.5	259.2
WV OK FL AZ GA MN MI UT KS NC	105.1	+9.9	76.7	298.7
MO PA CO OR WA ME IL VT VA OH	97.0	-6.4	69.6	305.7
NE CA MD MA NH CT NY DE NJ RI	81.9	-14.4	88.2	460.8

Figure 11.3: Voting Preference Based on Gun Ownership and BA Attainment

Gun ownership tends to be highest in rural areas. Educational advancement is generally higher in urban and suburban areas. The composite measure derived from these two demographic character-istics effectively segments voters in their candidate preferences in the 2016 presidential election. The states with higher composite scores, on average, favored Trump. Those with lower scores favored Clinton. This segmentation also demonstrates that the states that favored Clinton tended to be ones with larger populations and with stronger econo-mies. Localities negatively affected by globalization and technological advancements voted heavily for Trump.

These dramatic urban-rural differences have been noted by other observers. An issue of *The Economist* summarizes this reality: "rancorous political disputes—over guns, abortion, and climate change—split so neatly along urban-rural lines that parties and voters increasingly sort themselves into urban-rural tribes. Gerrymandering and party prima-ries reward extremists, and ensure that, once elected, they seldom need fear for their jobs."[3]

Trump's campaign message was focused on individuals whose eco-nomic fortunes had been devastated by static wages and reduced career opportunities. American companies have taken advantage of lower labor costs abroad to manufacture products more efficiently. Many Americans have lost high-paying jobs to foreign workers. As a group, these voters have less formal education and fewer skills that are appro-priate for the employment opportunities in our changing economy.

Trump's Electoral College victory resulted from winning the rust-belt states, including Pennsylvania, Ohio, Indiana, Michigan, and Wisconsin. Since 2001, the losses in manufacturing jobs have been 33 percent in Ohio, 33 percent in Michigan, 35 percent in Pennsylvania, 24 percent in Indiana, and 21 percent in Wisconsin. In prior elections, a majority of voters in these states preferred the Democratic candidate for president. By promising to introduce government policies that would create more traditional blue-collar jobs, Trump gained the support of many voters who had not previously cast their ballots for a Republican candidate. These employment opportunities, however, currently provide jobs for only 8.5 percent of American workers and account for only 12 percent of GDP.[4]

Trump's marketing genius connected in a visceral fashion to underemployed and unemployed workers. The promise to "Build the Wall" was a metaphor for removing foreign competition from the job market. The promise to erect tariffs on products from foreign countries addressed the same issue. The appeal to "Make America Great Again" and put "America First" addressed deeply felt resentment against the impact of globalization. Families that had lost a comfortable lifestyle needed to find a scapegoat. Washington politicians were an easy target. The phrase "Drain the Swamp" captured the imagination of millions. Trump understood the pain of those who had lost financially rewarding blue-collar jobs. His simplistic messages were marvelously effective.

The coalition that provided Trump's victory included voters that are not necessarily associated with standard Republican philosophy. For many years, the Republican party has advocated lower taxes and less federal involvement in the affairs of local communities. In addition, Republicans have been highly critical of a nanny government that limits individual freedoms, taxes those who are economically prosperous, and redistributes the money to those who are less successful.

An examination of where federal tax money is actually acquired and spent provides food for thought. The difference between the amount each state contributed in taxes to the federal coffers in 2012 and the federal expenditures that came back to each state provides an interesting economic analysis.[5] State differences were sorted from smallest to largest and listed in order from the ones that provided the largest subsidy to the federal government to those that received the largest financial benefits from the federal tax system. Figure 11.4 organizes these data in five groupings of ten states each. Average values on three relevant measures for each group are presented.

The Average Return per Dollar on Federal Taxes is a ratio of the money sent to Washington by each state divided by the amount received by each state. If a state receives as much as it contributes, this ratio would be 1.00. If a state receives less than it contributes, the ratio is less than 1.00. If a state receives more than it contributes, the ratio is more than 1.00. Figure 11.4 also provides the Average GDP for each group, a measure of its overall business activity. The third measure is the difference in votes received in the 2016 presidential election for each group between the two major candidates: the number of votes for Trump minus the number of votes for Clinton. A negative number indicates that Clinton received more votes than Trump among the ten states in the group. A positive number indicates that Trump received more votes than Clinton.

States	Avg Return per Dollar on Federal Taxes	Avg GDP (Billions $)	Trump Vote Advantage
NJ NV CT NH MN IL DE CA NY CO	0.73	645	-7,979,831
MA WI UT WA MI TX FL OR RI GA	0.93	516	-347,721
IN OH PA NC VT IA NE WY KS AZ	1.10	293	+1,911,878
ID TN MD MO SC OK AR ME HI MT	1.35	171	+1,734,704
KY VA SD AL ND WV LA AK MS NM	1.73	156	+2,080,103

Figure 11.4: Voting Preference Based on Economic Prosperity

Surprisingly, the states that voted heavily for the Democratic candidate are ones that send more money to Washington than they receive. The states that supported the Republican candidate enthusiastically were the ones that receive more money from Washington than they contribute in taxes. California, New York, New Jersey, Connecticut, and Illinois, all states that heavily favored Clinton, received, on average, 73 cents for every dollar they sent to Washington. Mississippi, Alaska, Louisiana, West Virginia, North Dakota, Alabama, South Dakota, and Kentucky voted overwhelmingly for Trump and on average received 1 dollar and 73 cents for every dollar they delivered to Washington. Rural areas and small-town America receive more in government services than they contribute in taxes to the national economy. Nonetheless, citizens in states receiving the greatest benefit from the federal tax system eagerly voted for the candidate who promised to change that system.

Republicans think of themselves as self-sufficient individuals that do not need government support to prosper in the American economy. The data just discussed, however, indicate that many of the states that voted for Trump and consistently favor Republican candidates for Congress are heavily subsidized by states that vote regularly for Democrats.

It is also clear that the states that voted most strongly for Clinton are the ones with the strongest economies.[6] The ten states at the top of the table had an average GDP of $645 billion. The ten states at the bottom had an average GDP of $156 billion. The economically successful states provided 8 million more votes for Clinton than for Trump. The states with the smallest economies provided an electoral edge for Trump of 2.1 million votes.

Trump promised to use government power to bring jobs back for people who were unemployed. His tariff proposal was designed to nullify the advantage of lower labor costs in other countries. Trump's plan to build a wall across our entire southern border was a plan for reducing job competition from Mexican migrants. He also proposed to increase government spending on infrastructure in order to create additional blue-collar jobs. All of these campaign promises were music to the ears of voters in the rust belt.

———

These four analyses comparing the demographic characteristics of different localities with voting preferences paint a fairly clear picture of which Americans were eager for change and ready to vote for Donald Trump. His voters tended to be white, older Americans living in rural or suburban areas. His supporters often resided in areas of the country that are not doing well economically. These localities are ones that have been harmed rather than helped by globalization and advancements in technology. Many of Trump's supporters appear to be people who would like to turn back the clock to a time when unsophisticated job skills were sufficient for gainful employment. Unfortunately for these voters, it is not likely that resurrecting the past will create more employment for Americans.

Chapter 12

————

FACING REALITY

Facts do not cease to exist just because they are ignored.
—ALDOUS HUXLEY

Government subsidies that provide a financial cushion for economically stressed areas of the country are not a long-term solution for declining employment prospects. However, subsidies can help communities break the poverty trap. It is unfortunate that local support of education in these impoverished communities is inadequate for what is needed. Affluent areas with superior funding provide residents with higher-quality instruction and training for modern jobs. These educational investments should be extended to less-wealthy communities to expand employment options.

Unfortunately, recent plans to alter our country's trade relationships with other nations may reduce employment opportunities. President Trump has introduced a 25 percent tariff on steel and a 10 percent tariff on aluminum that have been manufactured in factories on foreign soil.[1] American companies, such as those who manufacture consumer products or construct buildings, will be forced to raise prices. This will decrease the price competitiveness of these companies and very likely reduce production. It will put a damper on hiring and possibly lead to worker layoffs. American companies that efficiently produce products containing steel or aluminum will face difficulty selling their higher-priced products abroad.[2]

Renegotiating trade agreements, such as the North American Free Trade Agreement (NAFTA), could disrupt commerce that currently benefits American workers. In recent years, American refineries have expanded production of gasoline and diesel fuel for Mexican consumption.[3] Mexico has also become a major destination for surplus natural gas produced by the shale revolution. Sales south of the border have almost doubled since 2014. American oil and gas companies are planning to build additional pipelines into Mexico to double their sales over the next three years. Erecting tariffs could initiate a trade war that harms the American economy rather than helps it.

In a very real sense, a Republican president is proposing to improve employment opportunities for American workers by using the power of a nanny government to eliminate competition from foreign nations. These policies will negatively affect jobs in other parts of our economy and increase prices for American consumers. This is a perplexing policy for a Republican party that historically has presented itself as a champion of free trade. We live in a topsy-turvy world.

In the future, technology will continue to restructure commerce and advance the utility of globalization. Erecting impediments to global trade will produce more harm than benefit. Instituting tariffs on products manufactured by our current trading partners will not only raise prices locally but will also decrease competition and thereby reduce product quality and diversity. Free markets produce goods and services at the best prices. Items produced efficiently in other countries often become components of complex products assembled in this country. Tariffs would limit the opportunities for our businesses to acquire materials and special parts needed for the production of profitable items, like automobiles and trucks. If American companies have to acquire these components locally, their products may not be competitive in the global market. This would reduce profits and eliminate jobs.

Tariffs also inevitably induce retaliation, damaging the economy of all countries involved.[4] Generating an escalating trade war will limit

American opportunities to export goods and services. Foreign countries will react by placing tariffs on our agricultural products. This would be devastating for Midwestern farmers. If there is a trade war, the Americans most impacted by higher prices on basic family staples will be unemployed, including those who voted for Trump. The only people who will benefit will be those who live in nations that are not participating in the trade war.

Restricting global trade will be an economic disaster for both American consumers and corporate America. International commerce is a blessing, not a calamity. The American workplace is being destabilized primarily by technology rather than foreign workers or global trade. Tariffs may return production to America, but the new employees will be machines, not people. Economic nationalism will continue to accelerate automation. The average hourly compensation, including benefits, for manufacturing jobs in America is currently $37.71.[5] This number for Mexico is $5.90. For China, $4.12. For India, $1.59. Instead of reacting to trade restrictions by hiring American workers at $38 per hour, companies have a strong financial incentive to acquire machines that produce the same goods at a lower cost. Erecting tariffs will hasten the adoption of new manufacturing technologies rather than produce American jobs.

The president's promise to create "millions of manufacturing jobs" will be difficult to honor. Positions that require moderate technical skills are not likely to return to America. They have been devastated by novel techniques for improving productivity and reducing transportation costs. Factory jobs are being threatened by the rise of additive manufacturing—also called 3-D printing—in which sophisticated machines produce a wide range of products without the need for assembly workers. This novel technique can even be applied to forming biological tissue.[6]

Jobs in advanced manufacturing will provide attractive wages. These occupations, however, will require a relatively small number of workers who have sophisticated technical skills and the capability to adapt as production equipment evolves. These new manufacturing arrangements will employ computer-savvy techies rather than skilled machinists in overalls. An attempt to compete in a global economy by increasing the number of factory jobs for medium-skill workers will make American industry uncompetitive in the world of commerce.

Automation is already replacing American workers at a rapid pace. Banks now provide electronic banking. Taxis and delivery trucks will soon be displaced by driverless vehicles. The internet has diminished the need for telephones, radio, TV, books, magazines, newspapers, dictionaries, and encyclopedias. Many people who have built and serviced these amenities for years will soon be out of work. There is no way for Trump or anyone else to block the march of new technology. The promise of a middle-class income for most Americans is a covenant that will not be fulfilled by erecting trade barriers.

Midwestern farmers are more likely to be harmed if NAFTA is restructured or terminated. Currently America exports $39 billion in agricultural products. Some 30 percent of our farm trade is with Canada and Mexico.[7] American corn exports to these neighbors have increased sevenfold since 1994. Income from American beef exports to Mexico in 2016 exceeded $900 million. The Midwestern states that provided the margin of victory for Trump in the 2016 election could suffer significant economic damage if NAFTA is terminated. Whether this treaty can be renegotiated in a way that offers improvements for American business is unclear.

Trump's commitment to build a wall on our southern border will also fail to slay the forces of globalization. Although 63 million voters took his claims seriously, reality will necessarily raise its ugly head. Our nation exists in a modern world in which facts on the ground cannot be wished away. Technology, not trade, is the major disruptor of the world market. The magical solutions embedded in Trump's oratory will not abate the steady march of technical advancements.

Trump's tax revisions will not help Americans whose wages have been frozen or reduced. According to the nonpartisan Tax Policy Center, the recent tax legislation that was promoted as an across-the-board tax cut will have an anti-progressive effect.[8] In 2018, tax payers with an adjusted gross income (AGI) between $25,000 and $49,000 will receive an average reduction of $380. A middle-income family ($49,000 to $86,000) will have tax savings of $930. Upper-income families ($86,000 to $149,000) will pay $1,810 less. The wealthiest Americans (AGI more than $149,000) will average a tax savings of $7,460. In terms of dollars, 65.8 percent of the benefit from the new tax legislation will be enjoyed by those whose annual earnings exceed $149,000.

The gap in income between working Americans and business leaders is more likely to be reduced by classical economic factors. In a labor market with low unemployment, companies will necessarily have to compete for workers rather than workers competing for jobs. This should increase opportunities for wage growth and augment productivity. It should also provide a strong incentive for the adoption of new technologies.[9]

Since 2001, tax cuts by Republican administrations have added nearly $6 trillion to the national debt.[10] By 2025, the combined effect of these tax cuts will produce a reduction in government income of more than $10 trillion, with 20 percent of the money being retained by the top 1 percent of households.[11] Kevin Drum of *Mother Jones* has observed that the tax cuts since the year 2000 are responsible for almost as much as the entire federal deficit.

The primary beneficiaries of the US Treasury's loss of dollars will be those who can most easily contribute with minimal pain to our national budget.[12] The emphasis on enriching individuals who have been economically successful will exacerbate financial inequality. Reducing taxes on corporations and eliminating the estate tax will also selectively benefit affluent Americans. These changes will not produce more consumers, the essential ingredient for a healthy economy.

A recent analysis by the nonpartisan Congressional Budget Office indicated that 80 percent of the economic growth generated by these tax cuts will eventually benefit foreigners rather than American citizens because approximately one-third of our stock market is owned by foreign investors.[13] The new tax legislation will also not do much to help workers. With corporate tax savings in the bank, the Fortune 500 companies have invested thirty-seven times more money on stock buybacks than on increased wages for American workers.[14]

Trump's tax plan is essentially a modern implementation of Reagan's trickle-down economics. Reagan suggested that lower taxes on wealthy Americans should lead to more investment, a stronger economy, more jobs, and better incomes for workers. The implementation of this theory in the 1980s failed to produce the anticipated result. The gap between rich and poor continued to expand. According to *The Economist*, a recent sophisticated analysis by the OECD indicated that our tax system provides more favorable treatment for wealthy individuals than does that of Britain, Italy, Canada, France, or Germany.[15]

Altering our tax policy to favor the most fortunate few will provide precious little benefit for the individuals and families who are currently financially stressed. The new taxation program is a dreadful gift to our children and grandchildren. It will increase the national debt by more than one trillion dollars each year.

Donald Trump was prescient in recognizing the distress and anger of Americans who have been left behind by changing economic realities. Erecting trade barriers, however, in an attempt to reinstate obsolescent employment opportunities is sheer folly. Many jobs that were available to individuals with high school educations are now done by machines. Jobs in the fossil-fuel industry continue to be automated. Even in foreign nations, such as China, Japan, and India, the use of coal is being reduced. Efforts to resurrect outmoded jobs will be counterproductive. Our country needs to innovate. Trump should be an agent of change. The revisions that are required, however, do not include turning back the clock or isolating the American economy from the rest of the world. Globalization is here to stay.

If our scientists' predictions that increased levels of CO_2 and methane will gradually raise the global average temperature, job opportunities in many areas of the economy will increase. Geographic areas that formerly did not require central air conditioning will need additions of expensive equipment. Rising sea levels and more intense storms will mean that houses in low-lying coastal areas will have to be moved or demolished. Residents who have been displaced will need to seek new housing. As wind turbines and solar panels become more cost-efficient and the use of fossil fuels decreases, many new workers will be required to manufacture and install these twenty-first-century devices. There will be new jobs. Promulgating the idea that climate change is a hoax will delay programs to train our citizens for the jobs of the future.

Employment opportunities will move from the factory to marketing, sales, and human services. It may be necessary to modify established work routines. For example, retail and office work could operate twelve hours a day, six days a week. Two shifts of employees might work three days a week for twelve hours each. With this arrangement, workers would have shared responsibilities to cover the longer hours of operation. This might augment employment opportunities by as much as 50 percent. Putting more people to work with respectable salaries would provide a tremendous boost to the economy by substantially increasing the number of consumers. A company in New Zealand has recently experimented with a shorter workweek, with promising results.[16]

Working three days a week, people would have more time to engage in pastimes not related to work. This could lead to the creation of more jobs in education, recreation, and entertainment. It would also make sense to develop additional employment opportunities for child care and senior care. This is an area of our economy that is currently underfunded despite an obvious shortage of trained individuals with early education skills and others prepared to care for the elderly. In the future, our country will need fewer people working in production and more in human services. Historically, human service professions have not provided attractive salaries. This must change.

There is a natural tendency for humans to cling to established routines. It is comforting to believe that the behavior regularities of the past need not be changed. Rather than accept the reality of rapidly changing economic circumstances, we tend to engage in motivated reasoning. This takes several forms.[17] One is strategic ignorance, avoiding consideration of conflicting evidence. Another is simple rationalization in which we develop fanciful explanations for troubling counter examples. A third involves accepting the reality of the counter evidence but interpreting its impact in a manner that is consistent with preexisting beliefs. This counterproductive thinking hinders our ability to adjust constructively to the changing environment.

If we wish to maintain a healthy economy and an affluent middle class, we must adapt to new realities. Our government's top priorities should be improving our educational organizations and modernizing the transportation and communication systems that support and augment commerce. The United States must continue to lead the world, accepting an evolving work environment and adjusting our economy to compete successfully with other countries. The key to making America great again is to master new technologies and educate our young people to become leaders in the world of commerce. Attempts to close our borders, resurrect outdated manufacturing industries, and protect jobs in a dying fossil-fuel industry will damage our economy. A line from the film *The Quiet Man*, spoken by actor John Wayne, is highly relevant: "Life is hard, and it is harder if you are stupid."

———

We should welcome new technologies and global competition. What country is better prepared with human talent and capital resources to master the future? Americans have never been afraid to face the challenges of a new day. Does anyone believe that the march of tech-nology and globalization can be halted by the force of human will? Our Founding Fathers boldly created a novel governing system that has served us well. Isn't it time to reinvent our political system to address an evolving world of technological marvels?

Chapter 13

———

CLEAN-ENERGY TECHNOLOGY

What is more mortifying than missing the plum
for want of courage to shake the tree?
—LOGAN PEARSALL SMITH

Future realities can be better understood by examining how technological innovations are changing our economy and the workplace. Over the centuries, energy production has evolved. After many years of dependence on wood, the primary source became coal. The discovery of ample sources of oil in the twentieth century led to the widespread use of this fossil fuel. More recently, natural gas has become a competitive source of energy. These changes occurred primarily for financial reasons. Each new energy source was more cost-effective than its predecessors. The days are numbered for the widespread use of coal.[1] An additional benefit of these transitions is that natural gas creates only one-quarter as much carbon dioxide as coal and half as much as oil. In recent years, fracking of oil-laden shale, especially in America, has greatly increased the production of natural gas. Substituting gas for coal or oil greatly reduces harmful emissions. Less carbon in a fuel source reduces environmental damage.

Hydroelectric power, nuclear reactors, and new sources (such as wind and solar) produce essentially zero carbon dioxide and zero methane and are potentially more cost-effective than burning hydrocarbons. Currently, however, these renewables provide only 13 percent of our nation's electric power. This may change. Recent research and development has demonstrated that low-carbon approaches for creating electrical power are in an early stage of development.

New enhancements to green technologies are being announced on a monthly basis. More efficient systems and additional installations will increase output. Unlike hydrocarbons, sunlight and wind are available across the entire surface of our planet, providing many new locations for power generation. Decentralization of electricity creation will permit individual communities to have much greater control of this essential enterprise. Local management of the trade-off between a reliable energy supply and the protection of clean air and water will be a welcome development.

Scientists are enhancing the efficiency of solar cells. Depositing a copper oxide layer on top of regular solar cells offers a pathway for boosting energy conversion from today's 25 percent to a future value of 40 percent.[2] This change would be transformative because the added material is inexpensive. Recent research with cells made from perovskites foreshadows a possible less-expensive material for providing more cost-efficient energy conversion.[3] Solar cells can become a standard ingredient in roofing materials, making local energy production ubiquitous. In many parts of our country, electricity from solar panels is already more cost-effective than power from burning coal. We can have affordable energy without air pollution and without black lung disease.

Wind turbines are also being increased in height and blade size with efficiency improvements that are dramatic.[4] The largest turbines are being erected in offshore locations some 15 or 20 miles from land. In the Great Plains region, electricity from wind can be generated at two-thirds the cost of coal-fired power plants. As of August 2017, there were fifty-two thousand large wind turbines in forty-one states generating twice as much electricity as in 2010. Wind power in 2017 produced as much electrical power as hydroelectric dams and five times as much as the combined output of solar farms and rooftop solar installations.[5] Power generated from natural gas will soon be more expensive than electricity from green technologies. Fossil fuels may soon be abandoned not because of pollution problems but because they are not cost-effective.

The ideal locations for energy production are often located far from urban areas where most electricity is consumed. Wyoming has a plentiful supply of coal and wind energy. Arizona, New Mexico, Utah, California, and Nevada have desert areas that are optimal locations for solar farms. Many of the large cities where electrical energy is needed, however, such as New York, Philadelphia, Atlanta, Miami, and Chicago, are many miles distant from these sites. Current technology for transmission of electricity over long distances dissipates 30 percent or more of the energy. For this reason, coal is often transported by rail to power stations that are located near cities. Solar farms and wind farms are often located as close as possible to urban areas, despite the fact that these locations may not be optimal for energy production.

Recent advancements in transmission technology provide an opportunity to change the locations where electrical energy is generated. Ultra-high-voltage direct-current (UHVDC) transmission lines reduce energy loss and make long-distance transfers economical. China, with wind and solar energy resources within its interior and hydroelectric power in Tibet, has the capability of producing vast amounts of badly needed electrical energy. A difficulty, however, is that a large segment of China's population lives near the coast, far from these cost-effective sources of energy. It is not a surprise that China's state-owned electrical utility is investing $88 billion on UHVDC transmission lines over a ten-year construction period.[6]

This new transmission technology creates an opportunity for the United States to require coal-fired power plants to be sited in remote areas, such as Wyoming, where coal is plentiful. This removes the need to transport millions of tons of coal from where it is mined to power stations near urban areas. With UHVDC transmission, solar farms in remote areas of the Southwest can provide urban areas with electrical power at a competitive price. Wind turbines in Wyoming can also become a cost-effective source of power for large cities. Revolutionizing the nation's electrical grid in this manner would create jobs, reduce air pollution in cities, and lower electric bills for consumers. Technological advancements change our economy in many ways, destabilize established production methods, and force the development of new job skills by our workforce.

China is currently the world's largest importer of fossil fuels. Because of its dependence on "dirty" fuels, China is the planet's largest source of air pollution. In many cities, residents routinely wear air-filtering masks when they travel outdoors. To rectify this, China's leaders are establishing mandatory targets to roll back energy production from coal. The nation plans to generate 20 percent of its energy from green sources by 2030. China has pledged to invest one-third of a trillion dollars in solar, wind, hydro, and nuclear by 2020. This will create 10 million new jobs in China. Maybe we can learn something from our Asian neighbors.

ENERGY STORAGE SYSTEMS

A current drawback of generating electricity from wind and sunshine is that these sources of energy are highly variable. Sunshine is not available at night and is reduced on cloudy days, and wind is highly dependent on weather conditions. Often, green electricity production does not match the times of the day when demand is highest. Currently, fossil-fuel power stations need to be brought online to meet peak demand. Periodic use of these facilities is inefficient and expensive. What is needed is a method for storing the electricity produced by intermittent sources such as wind and solar. Combining an effective storage method with these environmentally friendly production systems could provide energy at lower cost than fossil fuels and generate much less damage to our planet's atmosphere.

Today's chemical batteries for storing electricity have a limited lifetime and are not particularly efficient in storing energy from a fluctuating source. However, recent research by Samsung has synthesized a graphene ball that permits lithium-ion batteries to hold 45 percent more energy and to be charged five times faster.[7] Graphene oxide supercapacitors also offer a novel technology for high-performance, low-cost energy storage.[8] These promising new methodologies have a superior ability to quickly charge and discharge energy and to store it longer without significant loss. Supercapacitors are also safer for use than chemical batteries because they can function without overheating, removing the danger of fire. Solar energy can also be captured in molten salt. High-temperature salt retains sufficient heat to power conventional turbines for generating electricity after the sun has set.

There have also been new discoveries in solid-state battery technology that seem very promising. One employs a magnesium-ion solid-state conductor as the electrolyte.[9] Another uses a specially formulated glass for the electrolyte.[10] Both of these advancements may lead to batteries with higher energy densities than lithium-ion batteries, a longer life cycle, nonflammability, faster charging times, and lower costs. Developing an improved electricity storage method will greatly increase the practicality of wind turbines and solar cells for energy production and will also make electrical vehicles more cost-competitive.

Other technological developments are offering additional possibilities for storing energy to cover demand when winds are calm and the sun is not present. Electrical energy, when demand is reduced, can be stored in private distributed storage systems. Home battery systems are becoming more affordable. The batteries of electric-powered automobiles that are garaged can capture solar power during the day and wind turbine power at night. Rooftop solar installations and small wind turbines can also be paired with local storage options. With generation and accumulation locally, the need for transmission lines, substations, and ugly utility poles can be reduced or even eliminated altogether.

A German energy company recently announced a plan with a university partner to build a massive flow battery in underground salt caverns.[11] A flow battery is a very large stationary battery that uses negatively and positively charged electrolyte pools to exchange electrons through an inexpensive membrane. Connected to the grid, this battery could power Berlin for an hour. Stanford scientists are developing a flow battery employing a liquid metal.[12] This research offers an approach that may provide high density at an attractive price without resorting to exotic chemicals or extreme temperatures.

Plans are also in place to pump water to reservoirs on elevated ground when wind and solar energy are plentiful. When demand exceeds production, water can be released to flow downhill, powering turbines and providing supplemental electric power. The economic case for building new power plants fueled by coal or gas is collapsing. New energy repositories, when engineered in the proper dimensions, will help eliminate the need for activation of fossil-fuel power stations when electrical demand peaks.

Electric vehicles (EVs) are becoming cost-competitive with traditional internal combustion vehicles. EVs have fewer than twenty moving parts, as compared to roughly two thousand in cars powered by internal combustion engines.[13] Maintenance costs will be reduced, and as EVs become mass-produced, manufacturing costs will also be diminished. Electricity for transportation can be generated without the use of fossil fuels. As the manufacture of EVs ramps up, there will be less demand for gasoline and diesel fuel and air pollution will decrease. In the future, the fossil-fuel industry will be hiring fewer workers.

It would be foolish to delay the inescapable transition to new energy sources for transportation. Although EVs currently make up less than 1 percent of the automobiles in America, industry experts anticipate a major rise in the number of EVs on the road in the second half of the 2020s. Almost all of the major car manufactures currently have aggressive development programs in place. Future batteries for EVs will have greater capacity for an equivalent weight and will be safer and less expensive. Anticipated improvements in electrical motor efficiency[14] will also make EVs more competitive with traditional transportation vehicles without the air pollution produced by internal combustion engines.

NUCLEAR POWER PLANTS

For reasons that have to do with historical realities, such as what happened at Hiroshima and Nagasaki, combined with our inability to comprehend the complexities of particle physics, humans have a natural aversion to creating electricity by nuclear fission. This is unfortunate. Electrical power generated from atomic reactions produces no carbon dioxide. It is not just a low-carbon technology. It is a zero-carbon technology.

It is not difficult to understand why humans dread the use of this technology. Images of giant fireballs easily come to mind. The historical reality is that nuclear reactors have a much better safety record than fossil fuels.[15] The air pollution produced by burning coal and gasoline has caused more harm to human health than any of the hazards associated with commercial atomic energy. The accident risk and the risk associated with environmental pollutants for nuclear reactors have been an order of magnitude less than that of our everyday fuels.

The high cost of nuclear reactors has been caused primarily by legislation that requires safety standards that greatly exceed those enforced for any other form of energy production. Their expense is also increased by the low production volume of these units. Fourth-generation reactors are constructed with designs that benefit from decades of research and implementation. They are more efficient, safer, and, when manufactured in quantity, less expensive than their predecessors. Many of these new designs are currently delivering relatively inexpensive electricity in France, Sweden, and South Korea.

As these new technologies come on line, the geographic location of power production will change, as will the skills that are required to operate and maintain these new facilities. Traditional blue-collar jobs in the rust belt are unlikely to make a comeback. The new opportunities for constructing solar farms will be in the Southwest, and the need for workers to build wind turbines will most likely be in mountainous areas and in the Great Plains. Nuclear facilities can be sited in remote areas, providing an additional degree of safety.

The occupational skills needed to build and maintain this new equipment will be different from those that have been a pathway for a middle-class income in previous years. Individuals seeking employment that pays well will need to relocate and acquire novel technical skills. "Go west, young man" may become sensible advice once again.

CLIMATE CHANGE

Trump's belief that our planet's weather is not changing is wishful thinking, a mental escape from reality. His proposal to reduce mileage requirements for vehicles that burn gasoline or diesel fuel will delay our nation's inevitable conversion to an automotive system based on electricity or hydrogen. Consuming greater quantities of fossil fuels will pollute the air our children breathe, result in higher prices for operating transportation vehicles, place us at risk with unreliable oil production by international partners, and increase our trade deficit.

We have benefited greatly from the environmental pioneers who have successfully lobbied legislative bodies. Our representatives have enacted regulations that have greatly enhanced the quality of the air we breathe and the water we drink. Our families enjoy natural habitats that were once seriously endangered. The technological ingenuity of our scientists has altered industry in a way that has cleared our skies and decontaminated our water. Environmental activism has been effective in influencing legislation that has preserved our nation's pristine biospheres. The ball, so to speak, is now in our court. Whether our generation will continue this laudatory record remains to be seen. The world our children and grandchildren inherit will depend on our choices.

Almost all scientists and many previous skeptics now believe that the destruction of carbon-consuming forests, the increase in carbon dioxide emissions from burning fossil fuels, and the release of methane by the warming of permafrost and discharges from cattle have contributed to global warming. The concentration of carbon dioxide in our atmosphere has increased from 270 parts per million prior to the industrial revolution to its current value at approximately 400 parts per million.[16]

Warming temperatures have melted sun-reflecting ice and snow in the Arctic regions. Newly exposed land and open water that absorb more sunlight have become the replacement. We are currently experiencing more severe weather, including droughts, heat waves, and more destructive hurricanes. To add to the calamity, the level of our oceans has increased almost 8 inches since 1870 and is continuing to rise.[17] Many large cities exist in locations that are only a few feet above sea level. Further rises in sea level will have a devastating effect on these urban populations. The cost of fortifying or moving commercial and residential buildings will be truly enormous: trillions of dollars.

Our challenge is clear. It is imperative for us to generate the energy we need without producing carbon dioxide and other environmentally damaging pollutants. We also need to develop engineering strategies that will reduce the concentration of carbon dioxide in our atmosphere. These will be difficult enterprises requiring ingenuity and major financial investments. Over the past five decades, we have reduced the creation of the five most noxious air pollutants by approximately 60 percent.[18] During these same years, the population of our country increased by more than 30 percent. This progress was the result of engineering enhancements that delivered more efficient industrial and automotive equipment and better emission control. These technological advancements continue to progress. We can be confident that our scientists and engineers will find new solutions for future environmental perils.

———

Our forefathers traveled across the Atlantic to found a new nation. Over the past 225 years, our predecessors have faced many challenges. The favorable status of our country today is a reflection of their arduous work, grave sacrifices, and political genius. It is time for us to look in a mirror and ask, "Can we do for our children and grandchildren what our parents and grandparents did for us?"

Chapter 14

―――

ENHANCING GENETIC INHERITANCE

It is not the strongest or the most intelligent who will survive but those who can best manage change.

— CHARLES DARWIN

When I was in middle school, our math teacher introduced the class to elementary algebra. For a few of us, understanding algebra was effortless. I ignored the teacher's lectures and proceeded to do the problems at the end of the chapter during class so I wouldn't have any homework. Some of my classmates, however, were baffled by the material. They struggled to do the algebra problems after school and sometimes gave up in frustration. At the time, I couldn't understand why such an easy assignment was so difficult for them.

In high school I encountered my first class in foreign language. I discovered that learning to understand and speak French was very challenging. Our teacher would assign new material each day and test us by reading French sentences from the appendix of the textbook and requiring us to write the sentence and provide a translation. For me, these tests were a disaster. My performance was miserable. I eventually earned a passing grade in the class by memorizing every sentence in the appendix. When my teacher spoke a French sentence, I was able to respond properly by identifying one or two of the words that were unique to that sentence. My classmates wondered why I was having so much difficulty with a task that was easily done by them.

In college, I had a friend who would listen to students from India, Italy, or Australia who spoke English with very distinct accents. He would then mimic their accents perfectly while discussing different subject matter. I could not understand how this was possible. Even if I practiced extensively, I could never have duplicated his exploit. My friend's talent, from my perspective, was nothing less than miraculous.

Clearly, we humans are different from each other in the aptitudes and talents we inherit from our parents. Genes actually matter. What is it about our genomes that make some of us proficient at scientific enterprises? As technology continues to alter our environment, wouldn't it be wonderful if all of us could master math, science, and engineering with ease? Our lives would be improved if everyone understood the mechanical realities of our transformed world.

The fundamental problem is the imperceptible rate at which the human genome adjusts to a changing environment. The skills that made our ancestors successful hunter-gatherers and subsequently productive farmers are no longer relevant in our modern society. The rise of intelligent machines has diminished the value of human proficiency at repetitive tasks. In the future, sales and marketing skills for engaging successfully in commerce will still provide a decent income. However, the individuals with aptitude and expertise for building and operating complicated machines will be the ones with high-paying jobs.

Many of our descendants will find themselves in an alien, bewildering world. Technical challenges will be perceived with frustration and resentment, often accompanied by personal feelings of inadequacy. The social repercussions are worrisome. Educational systems can be modified to provide knowledge that is relevant to what the future will require. Our children's and grandchildren's biological inheritance, however, cannot be so easily modified.

Can we surmount this troublesome transition? Recent history is not encouraging. Over the past several decades, the number of people with middle-class incomes has declined and the income gap between the well-to-do and the rest of the society has been steadily increasing. Those of us who were born with natural talent for dealing with machines are prospering. Those who are befuddled by technical devices are not.

THE GENETIC CODE

In 1953, James Watson and Francis Crick published a groundbreaking scientific paper describing the twisted-ladder structure of the DNA double helix.[1] Since then many contributors have shed light on the chemical process in which information in the DNA molecule is transferred to RNA (a similar molecule) and then employed to construct complex proteins that provide the structural constituents and metabolic processes that make life possible. The chemical complexity of these processes is sufficiently elaborate that scientists are still struggling today to understand the details.

The human genome contains approximately twenty thousand prescriptions for building complex biological molecules. Newborns receive half of these prescriptions from each parent. Genes provide information for building proteins. These macromolecules are long chains of twenty basic units. Proteins fold in complex ways, forming convoluted structures that induce chemical activity between two much smaller molecules. Essential biological chemical reactions would not occur without the catalytic activity of proteins.

Humans carry a common set of genes, but each gene comes in multiple forms. Some of these variations create a protein that produces biochemical activity that is different from what is produced by other variations of the same gene. These slight differences in the composition of each gene alter the proteins that are induced and thus alter body structure and essential metabolic processes. It is these multiple versions of each gene that make each of us unique. With twenty thousand genes and multiple variations of each one, the number of possible combinations is a colossal number. If one assumes that each gene, on average, has ten viable variations, the number of possible DNA sequences would be ten followed by twenty thousand zeros. That is an enormous number.

Occasionally, natural events cause a mutation, altering a gene and changing the protein created from the information that the gene normally carries. Often these changes have no physiological effect. Sometimes, however, the change can be harmful, eliminating a biochemical process that is necessary for an essential bodily function. The list of disorders produced by these rare mutations is very long.[2] Physiological impacts that can be observed early in childhood include autism, cystic fibrosis, hemophilia, and phenylketonuria. Other malfunctions can appear later in life, including Crohn's disease, muscular dystrophy, Parkinson's disease, Tay-Sachs syndrome, and sickle cell disease. Common cancers also have a genetic component and are often observed to run in families. These include breast cancer, prostate cancer, and colon cancer. There are also other genetically determined illnesses that are extremely rare and very bizarre. One of these is heterotaxy syndrome in which internal organs are malformed, missing, multiplied, or misplaced. The negative impact of these afflictions on individuals and families can be devastating.

Recently, biochemists have discovered a natural process in bacteria that protects them from attacks by viruses. Bacteria fight these invaders by severing and thus destroying viral DNA. The protein CRISPR-Cas9 is an enzyme produced by bacteria that allow them to disable foreign DNA. Biochemists have adapted this enzyme for laboratory use.[3] Scientists have also devised procedures to synthesize RNA strands in the laboratory that can recognize specific sequences (typically about twenty units long) that permit targeting of locations along the DNA strand. The combination of these two advances provides molecular scissors that can cut DNA at a specific location. When DNA is cut, the cell recognizes the damage and attempts to repair it. This provides an opportunity to insert a new component to the DNA string. By employing this method, geneticists can precisely edit a specific section of a DNA chain. This permits the replacement of a defective gene with one that functions properly, eliminating once and forever the terrible illness produced by the defective gene.

As these novel techniques mature and are refined for general use by the medical community, a wide range of genetic diseases can be eliminated from the human genome. No longer will the victims be susceptible to the damaging effect of a harmful mutation. In addition, his or her germ cells will not pass the defect to subsequent generations. This is a wonderful example of how advanced technologies can have a major beneficial impact on millions of human lives.

Scientists have focused their research with these new genetic tools on serious medical problems that cannot be addressed with surgical or pharmaceutical treatments. These tools may also provide a method to address the growing disparity between the rush of technological innovation and humanity's inability to acquire new employment skills rapidly enough to keep pace. The selective capability to modify DNA may provide a solution. It could empower prospective parents to employ gene manipulation to enhance their offspring's aptitudes. This possibility is provocative and encouraging.

Medical procedures that replace a defective gene with an effective one using the CRISPR-Cas9 methodology usually depend on repairing a single gene. For many maladies, geneticists have already identified the defective gene. Being able to influence complex behavioral traits, however, would require modification of more than one gene. Determining the DNA segments that are related to specific aptitudes will be arduous. Nonetheless, inducing minor variations in a half dozen or more genes might impact biochemical activity in a way that facilitates technical proficiencies required for employment in the future. Minor modifications may provide a child with a capability that neither parent possesses. In every other respect, the child would inherit the family characteristics normally conveyed by his or her parents.

One might wonder if this is just wishful thinking. Is it science fiction rather than a realistic vision of the future? Is it possible to make subtle changes in our children's genomes that provide desirable aptitude enhancements? Can we imagine a world in which all of our young people easily master computers and complex electronic equipment?

There are two essential objectives that must be realized. One is an improvement in our understanding of genetic inheritance. Scientists will need to unravel the complexity of the DNA chain to identify gene combinations that are associated with specific physical or mental aptitudes. With twenty thousand genes and multiple variants for each one, the number of possible combinations is gigantic: hundreds of trillions. Finding a particular combination associated with engineering talent or computer programming aptitude would be a formidable challenge. Understanding why some individuals are more gifted than most people in solving technical dilemmas, generating complex computer software, or solving mathematical brainteasers would be an amazing achievement.

More than fifty years ago, psychologists developed a paper-and-pencil test to measure a person's mental ability to rotate three-dimensional images. The subjects are shown a depiction of an alarm clock. Directions are then given to imagine several rotations of the object. For example, "Mentally rotate the clock 90 degrees to the right, then tip the top forward 270 degrees, and finally rotate the object 45 degrees to the left." The subject is then presented with four three-dimensional drawings of a clock and asked to select the one that represents the position that would be reached after the requested movements have been made.[4] Some people select the correct orientation correctly without difficultly. Others are hopeless at this task. Psychologists have discovered that individuals that do this task well are more likely to become successful engineers than subjects who perform poorly.

Consider an example of how a person's genes might be related to this behavioral trait. Individuals having variant 12 of gene 759 combined with variant 7 of gene 1,265, variant 15 of gene 13,458, and variant 3 of gene 16,374 may have little difficulty mentally rotating objects. It follows that the individuals who have these particular variants of these four genes would be more likely to be successful engineers. The challenge, of course, is finding a way to discover these relationships. Is it possible to uncover a large number of genetic patterns that are each associated with specific desirable talents?

Developments in computer power, memory capacity, and sophisticated software have provided data-analytic capabilities that until recently only existed in science fiction novels. Today machines can examine millions of complex records and discover elaborate patterns that occur infrequently. As more people submit saliva samples to be screened for a complete DNA analysis, researchers can construct a colossal database containing detailed information regarding each person's genetic inheritance. With tens of millions of samples and with detailed physical and behavioral information for each person, scientists can uncover relationships between specific genetic patterns and human physical and mental aptitudes. These patterns are likely to be highly elaborate. An advantageous behavioral trait could involve specific molecular variants (alleles) of six or more genes.

The second indispensable ingredient would be the dissemination of the CRISPR-Cas9 methodology broadly throughout our medical communities. This technique will permit the modification of genes by substituting one variant (allele) for another. Each of the critical genes would be replaced by a slightly different version. The anticipated result would be an enhancement of a specific aptitude, such as numerical reasoning or mechanical cleverness. Could one actually conceive a child that looks and behaves like his or her parents and grandparents but is more technically proficient than any of them? Might it be possible to make minor DNA changes that improve a child's ability to develop the skill sets needed for success in the twenty-first century?

FUTURE PROSPECTS

For many of us, these possibilities conjure up thoughts of an unnatural future world, foreshadowing unknown consequences. There is a different perspective, however. Those of us who accept Darwin's theory of evolution can regard the development of this proposed technology as just one in a long series of events that have altered our species over multiple centuries. Many scientists believe that humans have evolved from more primitive organisms and are still evolving at an imperceptible pace. The capability to make minor changes in several genes might provide a tool for giving the evolutionary process a helping hand. For the first time, we may not have to rely on random events that alter the human genome and then depend on the rule of tooth and claw to select those variations that augment survival.

Instead, we could increase the frequency of genetic variations that conquer the challenges of our modern environment. Alterations fabricated with this novel technique would be passed on to future generations. In a very real sense, this new technology would accelerate a natural process that has created the biological tissue we now inhabit. By enhancing the pace of adaptation to our changing environment, humanity will be more likely to prosper in the unfamiliar world of the future. We should not fear these new genetic tools. Instead, it would be more appropriate to celebrate their discovery. In their absence, our children and grandchildren and their progeny could face a bewildering, problematic world.

In the years to come, prospective parents might select particular behavioral aptitudes that they would prefer their children to have. They might choose among many possibilities. The menu could include musical talent, athletic prowess, engineering aptitude, verbal facility, and many other capabilities. Would it be wrong for parents to enhance their children's genome? Why not provide our children with the aptitudes required to succeed in the world of the future?

It is likely that cautious people will view this possible voluntary option with great consternation. The world's religions presume our planet and all of its life-forms were created by a Supreme Being. The idea that humanity might alter the fundamental processes that have characterized life on this planet for millions of years is a prospect that many people may view with horror. They might believe this proposal is an appalling disruption of the preordained order.

Instead, however, humanity may have been blessed with intelligence in order to persevere in an evolving world. To prosper in the future, humans will need to master increasingly complex machines. If our world has been created by a Supreme Being, he or she probably anticipated the alterations in humanity's capabilities that would be necessary for survival. Isn't it possible that the development of powerful computational devices and the discovery of the CRISPR-Cas9 gene in bacteria might have been part of the Supreme Being's original plan?

Chapter 15

———

A COMPREHENSIVE PLAN

The probability that we might fail in the struggle should not deter us from support of a cause we believe to be just.

—ABRAHAM LINCOLN

At the beginning of the twenty-first century, our nation suffered a devastating terrorist attack that killed nearly three thousand Americans. We responded by attacking Iraq, killing tens of thousands of people, and creating a political vacuum that has been populated by terrorists, dictators, and incompetent politicians. The Iraq War was followed by the worst financial crisis our country had faced in eighty years. The war expenditures and the financial investments that were needed to rebuild our economy after the housing debacle have greatly exacerbated our government's debt.

Disastrous decisions in Washington have been accompanied by a degree of political corruption that has not been seen in a century. Powerful corporate interests dominate the legislative process. The laws that have recently been enacted do not address our country's central problems. Instead they mostly provide targeted benefits for those with sufficient resources to finance political campaigns. Recent polls have consistently demonstrated that a majority of the American public

favors increased spending on transportation infrastructure, lower interest charges on student loans, an increased federal minimum wage, and
action to fight climate change by reducing carbon emissions. Congress
has failed to address these concerns, even though each issue provides
an opportunity for governmental progress. Our legislators are more
concerned with who takes credit for improvements than with actually
accomplishing desirable reforms.

Historical observations lead one to believe that our political system
is gradually changing into a plutocracy in which wealthy individuals
dominate political decision making. The nation appears to be adopting
a libertarian philosophy in which freedom means that powerful people
have the right to manipulate our governmental processes for their own
benefit. By fostering self-serving legislation, individuals and corporations with abundant financial resources are compromising governmental decisions. It is not surprising that millennials associate business with
unscrupulous activities rather than honest competition. A recent poll by
Frank Luntz, a Republican, found that only 6 percent of respondents
in the 18–26 age group admired business people.[1] Americans are dis-
gusted that chief executives of major corporations make three hundred
times as much as average workers. Something is seriously wrong when
52 percent of recent GDP gains go to the top 1 percent.[2] Enlightened
leadership is needed to recapture the American dream.

Some of us believe that our country would be more prosperous and
more influential internationally if we had autocratic leadership. Do we
need someone who can make the tough decisions and cut through red
tape in order to fix the current mess in Washington? Strong leaders in
other countries are able to confront problems promptly and efficaciously.
Vladimir Putin in Russia, Xi Jinping in China, and Recep Tayyip Erdo-
gan in Turkey provide strong leadership without the discord and dysfunction that characterizes our democracy. In the 2016 presidential election,
the candidate representing the Republican party advocated greater
emphasis on bold, robust leadership. Donald Trump, our president and

a businessman, believes that our country would function more effectively with a president who emulates a corporate CEO.

History demonstrates, however, that authoritarian leadership, in the absence of constitutional restraints, produces corrupt tyrants. Many years ago, Alexis de Toqueville identified the hazard of unrestrained executive power: "A nation that asks nothing of government but the maintenance of order is already a slave in the depths of its heart; it is a slave of its well-being, ready for the man who will put it in chains."[3] Winston Churchill pinpointed the dilemma: "It has been said that democracy is the worst form of government except for all those other forms that have been tried."[4]

Other Americans believe that our country would be better if we did not have a federal government. The reality is that government is necessary for society to function. Former Republican senator and secretary of defense Bill Cohen once said, "Government is the enemy, until you need a friend."[5] Unrestrained liberty leads to theft and violence. Unrestrained government leads to corruption and injustice. A delicate balance is needed to create a society that fosters freedom and economic prosperity for everyone.

The dual nature of our republic—individual liberty combined with community responsibility—was emphasized by Bill Clinton.[6] He pointed to the two sides of our humble penny: "On one side, next to Lincoln's portrait is a single word: 'Liberty.' On the other side is our national motto. It says, 'E Pluribus Unum'—'Out of Many, One.' It does not say, 'Every man for himself.'" The success of our country depends on our commitment to live in harmony with our neighbors as well as to honor each individual's basic rights. As Clinton said, "These two commitments—to protect personal freedom and to seek common ground—are the coin of our realm, the measure of our worth."

In 1991, Clinton offered a vision for progress: "Our burden is to give people a new choice, rooted in old values, a new choice that is simple, that offers opportunity, demands responsibility, gives citizens more say, provides them responsive government—all because we recognize that we are a community, we are all in this together, and we are going up or down together."[7]

Many years ago, Justice William Brennan asserted, "The genius of the Constitution rests not in any static meaning it might have had in a world dead and gone, but in the adaptability of its great principles to cope with current problems and current needs."[8] There is also a French Proverb that says, "Only that which is provisional endures." To conserve the brilliant work of our Founding Fathers, we must adapt their ideas to our modern world. They would hardly recognize the planet on which we live today. Technology has dramatically altered transportation, communication, and manufacturing possibilities. There has been a revolution in attitudes regarding race, religion, and social mores. Why would any rational person believe that the Founders, no matter how gifted, could have created 225 years ago a governmental structure that is optimal for our modern world?

Human nature tends to resist change. We all are comfortable with an environment that is familiar. This aspect of our character is aptly captured by a familiar refrain: "Better the devil you know than one you don't know." Putting up with a bad situation because one fears what might follow inhibits the desire to seek improvements. Revolutions are frightening. Even minor modifications can make people nervous. Changing the structure of our government will be difficult.

LEGISLATIVE ACTION

Many of the innovations that I have proposed can be achieved by acts of the legislatures. The three major reforms that are most essential can be enacted by Congress and the president. These are the universal safety net, health service accounts, and modernization of our military forces. The implementation of a basic living stipend for all citizens over the age of seventeen will replace a huge bureaucracy of overlapping and inefficient government programs and eliminate the personal stigma associated with receiving federal financial support. This transition will augment consumer activity and enhance the national economy. Establishing a market-based universal health care system will improve the lives of millions of Americans and reduce the excessive federal medical expenditures that threaten to bankrupt our union. Improving our military forces while decreasing the number of young people in harm's way will enhance our preparedness to defend the nation. By modernizing our military forces, we can reduce expenditures and be better prepared to mitigate future existential threats.

These adjustments will have major economic benefits and will greatly improve the functionality and efficiency of government operations. The net budgetary impact of these changes will provide additional resources for repairing our crumbling infrastructure and reforming our outdated public education system. Preparing our nation to be competitive in the emerging global economy should be one of our top priorities. Developing a knowledgeable workforce and providing exceptional communication and transportation systems are essential for maintaining our preeminence in the world of commerce. History provides a wealth of evidence that international business activity elevates everyone's standard of living and provides a powerful antidote to warfare.

Congress and the President can also institute refinements that provide more opportunity for individuals to engage in economic activity on a level playing field. Legislation that favors major corporations at the expense of small businesses should be eliminated. Rules that limit fair competition hinder our economy and bestow an unnecessary burden on innovative new businesses. Patent law has become a serious barrier hindering the development of ingenious new products. Government regulations should encourage inventions, not provide an environment in which technological enhancements are restricted by lawyers working for giant corporations.

Legislation could also reform the tax code. The elimination of adjustments and deductions that benefit special interests would simplify tax preparation and would provide evenhanded, impartial taxation that ends targeted advantages for people and organizations with political clout. Creating a more progressive tax code would also make the system more equitable. Those who benefit most from a well-organized economy should be asked to contribute more.

Our legislators should also fund government agencies that enforce our laws and regulations. Underfunding the Internal Revenue Service encourages tax evasion. When everyone is not required to pay their fair share, the nation's income suffers. A tax system that balances income and spending is necessary. Congress continues to borrow money to provide benefits for seniors today and expects the bill to be paid by their children and grandchildren tomorrow. Operating the nation on deficit budgeting is unsustainable.

ELIMINATING THE ELECTORAL COLLEGE

Eliminating the Electoral College would make the election of our president more democratic. Voters in a majority of our states are aware that the outcome for the election of the president in their state is highly likely to be the same as in previous elections, whether or not they cast a ballot. In recent years, the result of the presidential contest has been determined by the outcome in eleven "toss-up" states. This provides very little incentive for voters in traditionally blue states or red states to cast a vote. This reality suppresses voter turnout and seriously compromises our voting system. The winner should be selected on the basis of the national popular vote. Since every vote would count, it is likely that more people would be engaged in the election.

It is interesting to note that the United States is an extreme outlier in its method for selecting its head of state. In the world's other fifty-eight democracies, the winner is the candidate who receives the most popular votes.[9] America is the only country on the planet in which a candidate who receives almost three million more votes is declared the loser.

Fortunately, eliminating the Electoral College can be done by state legislators. Electoral votes are cast by individual states based on rules established by each state. Currently, the candidate winning the popular vote in each state receives all of the state's electoral votes. The exceptions are Maine and Nebraska, where the winners in separate geographic districts determine how the electoral votes are allocated. Each state, however, has the option of altering the way its electoral votes are cast.

An intriguing proposal is for each state to cast all of its electoral votes for the presidential candidate that receives the most votes on a national basis. If states with a cumulative total greater than 270 votes decided to adopt this procedure, the candidate who won the national popular vote would become president. This would eliminate the unique and antiquated process developed by our Founding Fathers as a necessary but unfortunate action to gain acceptance of the constitution in 1787. This change would make the presidential election conform to the principle of one-person, one-vote. The candidate who received the most popular votes would be the winner.

In recent national elections, there have been fourteen states and the District of Columbia that have reliably voted for the Democratic candidate for president. Together, these regional areas have 193 electoral votes. There have been twenty-five states that have consistently voted for the Republican candidate. These states have a total of 212 electoral votes. The remaining eleven states, the "toss-up" states—Florida, Pennsylvania, Ohio, Michigan, Virginia, Wisconsin, Colorado, Nevada, Maine, New Hampshire, and Iowa—have voted less predictably. Collectively, these states have 135 electoral votes.

In order to enact changes that eliminate the Electoral College, it would be necessary for legislators in states that collectively have more than 270 electoral votes to cast them for the winner of the national popular vote. It is not likely that Republican states would endorse this change since they benefit substantially from the Electoral College arrangement. To originate a change, it would be necessary for all of the states that are reliably Democratic to cast their votes (193) in favor and also necessary for a subset of the eleven toss-up states to do so to provide another 78 votes. If Florida, Pennsylvania, and Ohio (67 votes) were joined by Michigan (16 votes) or Virginia (13 votes) or Nevada and Iowa (12 votes) or Wisconsin and Colorado (19 votes), the proposed modification would take effect. Currently, the District of Columbia and states representing 169 votes have endorsed this plan: California, Connecticut, Hawaii, Illinois, Maryland, Massachusetts, New Jersey, New York, Rhode Island, Vermont, and Washington.

It is worth noting that if this modification for casting electoral votes had been adopted prior to the national election in 2000, Albert Gore would have become president. Gore had a half million more votes than Bush. In the 2016 election, Hillary Clinton would have won. She had almost three million more votes than Trump.

MODIFYING THE CONSTITUTION

Many of the changes I have advocated will require amendments to the Constitution. Article Five of the Constitution requires a two-thirds vote of both federal legislatures or an affirmative vote by two-thirds of the states to propose an amendment. In addition, whatever is proposed must be ratified by three-quarters of the states.

The only amendments ratified in recent years are ones that provide small refinements to our governmental processes. The Twenty-Seventh Amendment, ratified in 1992, required increases in legislators' salaries to take effect after the next election. The Twenty-Sixth Amendment, ratified in 1971, reduced eligibility for voting from twenty-one years to eighteen years. The Twenty-Fifth Amendment, ratified in 1967, dealt with provisions for filling vacancies in the office of president and vice president caused by death, resignation, or removal from office. History demonstrates that even highly popular amendments such as these have taken years for passage.

The most sensible strategy for promoting constitutional corrections would be to attack the problem at its core. The first effort should be to change the way we amend the Constitution of the United States. We could retain the two-thirds vote by both legislatures or the affirmative vote by two-thirds of the states for proposing an amendment. We could replace ratification by three-quarters of the states by a simple up-or-down vote by the president. This would greatly simplify the amendment process and enable our country to address modifications that are long overdue. This transformative innovation could be enacted with a single constitutional amendment.

The most important proposals in this book that would require amendments to the Constitution for implementation are (1) altering the number of senators from twenty of the states, (2) setting new standards for redistricting the House, (3) permitting the legislatures with agreement from the president to overrule the Supreme Court, (4) enacting federal standards for voter eligibility, and (5) requiring all states to adopt new procedures for federal primary elections. Under the current provisions for amending the Constitution, one wonders if any of these actions could be proposed and ratified. A rational person setting betting odds would consider each of these modifications to be a long shot.

ALTERING SENATE REPRESENTATION

Increasing the number of senators from the ten states with the largest populations and decreasing the number from the ten states with the smallest populations would rationalize power relationships in Washington without completely abandoning the original intentions of our Founding Fathers. The intention in 1787 was to provide more legislative influence for states with smaller populations by creating a second legislative body, the Senate, in which the number of residents in the state did not influence voting power. My proposal maintains this intention but diminishes its enormously enhanced impact because, over time, there has been a massive divergence in state populations. I believe the compromise reached in 1787 would have been quite different if the authors of the Constitution had known that state population differences would increase in size to a ratio of 68 to 1 between the largest state and the smallest state.

REDISTRICTING THE HOUSE

The number one enemy of an impartial political system is the current procedure for redistricting the House of Representatives. The creation of safe House districts by state legislative action using modern technology has created a bizarre patchwork of gerrymandered districts. Every two years, our nation has a national election to select representatives to the House. Currently most of the districts have been carefully constructed to be "safe" for one of the two major political parties. With only thirty or so competitive districts, voters have minimal influence on who gets elected. This is an egregious violation of the Founding Fathers' intention. This intolerable arrangement has to be corrected.

The benefit of making our voting system more in line with a one-person, one-vote arrangement would seem to be obvious. As noted in *The Economist*, "Systems with elements of proportional representation, such as that sought by reformers of the electoral college or House districts, not only provide bulwarks against charges of illegitimacy. They also have a tendency towards consensus of the sort the founders wanted."[10]

OVERRULING THE SUPREME COURT

Our legal system is based on the premise that a governmental system can be established that provides a permanent standard for how a country should be administered and regulated. In 1787, the affairs of humanity transpired in a way that was very similar from one generation to the next. This is no longer true. If a person who was alive at the time when the Constitution was written visited us today, he or she would be astounded and disoriented.

Adhering to an inflexible system created on precedents established in an earlier era has produced legal decisions that are less than optimal. Determinations that are based on outdated precedents may be inappropriate for the realities of our present world.

Attempting to change our legal system would be extremely difficult and terribly disruptive. A reasonable alternative would be to permit action by the House, the Senate, and the president to overrule unsuitable Supreme Court decisions.

FEDERAL STANDARDS FOR VOTING

Currently, each of the fifty states determines who is eligible to vote, how the votes can be cast, and where and when voting will take place. There needs to be a uniform set of federal regulations. Every citizen over seventeen years of age should be able to cast a ballot in federal elections. It is reprehensible that state legislatures can currently restrict voting privileges for the purpose of partisan advantage. Voter suppression has become a standard ploy for biasing the outcome of elections. Citizens that prefer candidates from the political party that is not in control of the state legislature are systematically prevented from voting. This is completely inconsistent with the premise that every citizen should have the right to participate in our political system.

NONPARTISAN PRIMARIES

It would be beneficial to have a single primary election in each state that is organized and controlled by a neutral election board. The two major parties should have no more authority than any other organization in recommending candidates. Primary voting should employ the Approval Voting method. The general election would be a contest between the two candidates with the highest approval votes in the primary. Removing the two major parties' tyrannical control of candidate selection would be a monumental enhancement of our political process.

———

Taking action to fix our broken political system only after a serious crisis develops is an ineffective way to govern. The United States will continue to experience discord and dysfunction unless voters focus on corrective actions. Belatedly adopting incremental changes has created the disarray we face today. Our problems in recent years have a simple explanation: Our society lacks an effective political system that can bolster social well-being and economic prosperity for all Americans.

It is time to confront reality and enact major refinements in the structure of a government that was created by a small group of courageous and brilliant individuals more than two centuries ago. This will be an arduous task. Voters have busy lives with responsibilities and interests that direct their attention to work and family. Issues such as politics and government are not an immediate priority. In addition, there is always uneasiness in adopting unfamiliar proposals that require novel thinking. Most people are comfortable with habitual attitudes and daily routines.

Acceptance of a transformation in the way we are governed is comparable to the way people recognize a novel scientific finding. Max Planck, the originator of quantum theory, reflected on humanity's tendency to reject change: "A new scientific truth does not triumph by convincing its opponents and making them see the light, but rather because its opponents die, and a new generation grows up, that is familiar with it."[11]

This mission will take organizational skill, dedication, and ceaseless effort. Hopefully, we can introduce improvements before our country's most senior generation departs. We should be inspired by a simple truth: "Begin, the rest is easy."

If not now, when?

APPENDIX:
RETIREMENT INCOME
PROJECTION

A ssume at retirement age the accumulated savings for retirement will be based on two people. Either each person is married or is living with another person. Additions to the retirement account are therefore based on the income of two people.

Assume that each person earns $6,000 a year during the summer and vacation periods during ages 18–21. At age 22, each person earns $15 per hour. Annual income increases each year, on average, by 2 percent until age 50. Between 50 and 59, income increases by 1 percent. At 60 and after, annual income is static. Note that college grads at age 22 are likely to earn more than $15 per hour. The projected income assumptions are intentionally conservative because both individuals may have periods of time when they are not employed.

Each employee and each employer contributes 2.5 percent to the employee's retirement account. Thus, the retirement contributions are 5 percent each year.

At age 40, each person begins to set aside 5 percent of his or her income in a personal retirement account.

The funds in the retirement accounts grow each year by 6 percent. Historical records indicate that over time equity investments average a 10 percent annual increase. The 6 percent assumption is therefore conservative.

Both people retire at age 68 and begin withdrawals from their joint retirement accounts. This assumption is an approximation since the two people may not be of the same age.

Financial advisors suggest that retirement income should be approximately 70 percent of preretirement income. The assumption of $96,000 a year is 81.5 percent of the two people's income at age 67.

Age	2-Person Universal Stipend	2-Person Annual Earnings	Mandatory Retirement Contribution	Retirement Accumulation	Cumulative Personal Savings	2-Person Retirement Funds	Retirement Withdrawals
18	19,200	12,000	600	600	0	600	0
19	19,200	12,000	600	1,236	0	1,236	0
20	19,200	12,000	600	1,910	0	1,910	0
21	19,200	12,000	600	2,625	0	2,625	0
22	19,200	62,400	3,120	5,902	0	5,902	0
23	19,200	63,648	3,182	9,439	0	9,439	0
24	19,200	64,921	3,246	13,251	0	13,251	0
25	19,200	66,219	3,311	17,357	0	17,357	0
26	19,200	67,544	3,377	21,776	0	21,776	0
27	19,200	68,895	3,445	26,527	0	26,527	0
28	19,200	70,273	3,514	31,632	0	31,632	0
29	19,200	71,678	3,584	37,114	0	37,114	0
30	19,200	73,112	3,656	42,997	0	42,997	0
31	19,200	74,574	3,729	49,305	0	49,305	0
32	19,200	76,065	3,803	56,067	0	56,067	0
33	19,200	77,587	3,879	63,310	0	63,310	0
34	19,200	79,138	3,957	71,066	0	71,066	0
35	19,200	80,721	4,036	79,366	0	79,366	0
36	19,200	82,335	4,117	88,244	0	88,244	0
37	19,200	83,982	4,199	97,738	0	97,738	0
38	19,200	85,662	4,283	107,885	0	107,885	0
39	19,200	87,375	4,369	118,727	0	118,727	0
40	19,200	89,123	4,456	130,307	0	130,307	0
41	19,200	90,905	4,545	142,671	4,545	147,216	0
42	19,200	92,723	4,636	155,867	9,454	165,321	0
43	19,200	94,578	4,729	169,948	14,750	184,698	0
44	19,200	96,469	4,823	184,968	20,459	205,427	0

Age	2-Person Universal Stipend	2-Person Annual Earnings	Mandatory Retirement Contribution	Retirement Accumula-tion	Cumulative Personal Savings	2-Person Retirement Funds	Retirement Withdrawals
45	19,200	98,399	4,920	200,986	26,606	227,592	0
46	19,200	100,366	5,018	218,064	33,221	251,285	0
47	19,200	102,374	5,119	236,266	40,333	276,599	0
48	19,200	104,421	5,221	255,663	47,974	303,637	0
49	19,200	106,510	5,325	276,329	56,178	332,506	0
50	19,200	107,575	5,379	298,287	64,927	363,214	0
51	19,200	108,651	5,433	321,617	74,255	395,872	0
52	19,200	109,737	5,487	346,401	84,197	430,598	0
53	19,200	110,834	5,542	372,727	94,791	467,518	0
54	19,200	111,943	5,597	400,687	106,076	506,763	0
55	19,200	113,062	5,653	430,382	118,093	548,475	0
56	19,200	114,193	5,710	461,914	130,889	592,803	0
57	19,200	115,335	5,767	495,396	144,509	639,904	0
58	19,200	116,488	5,824	530,944	159,004	689,947	0
59	19,200	117,653	5,883	568,683	174,426	743,110	0
60	19,200	117,653	5,883	608,687	190,775	799,461	0
61	19,200	117,653	5,883	651,091	208,104	859,194	0
62	19,200	117,653	5,883	696,039	226,473	922,511	0
63	19,200	117,653	5,883	743,684	245,944	989,627	0
64	19,200	117,653	5,883	794,187	266,583	1,060,770	0
65	19,200	117,653	5,883	847,721	288,461	1,136,182	0
66	19,200	117,653	5,883	904,467	311,651	1,216,118	0
67	19,200	117,653	5,883	964,618	336,232	1,300,850	0
68	19,200					1,359,076	96,000
69	19,200					1,321,608	96,000
70	19,200					1,283,016	96,000
71	19,200					1,243,267	96,000
72	19,200					1,202,325	96,000
73	19,200					1,160,155	96,000
74	19,200					1,116,719	96,000
75	19,200					1,071,981	96,000
76	19,200					1,025,900	96,000

Continued

Age	2-Person Universal Stipend	2-Person Annual Earnings	Mandatory Retirement Contribution	Retirement Accumula- tion	Cumulative Personal Savings	2-Person Retirement Funds	Retirement Withdrawals
77	19,200					978,437	96,000
78	19,200					929,550	96,000
79	19,200					879,197	96,000
80	19,200					827,333	96,000
81	19,200					773,913	96,000
82	19,200					718,890	96,000
83	19,200					662,217	96,000
84	19,200					603,843	96,000
85	19,200					543,719	96,000
86	19,200					481,790	96,000
87	19,200					418,004	96,000
88	19,200					352,304	96,000
89	19,200					284,633	96,000
90	19,200					214,932	96,000
91	19,200					143,140	96,000
92	19,200					69,194	96,000
93	19,200					0	88,394
94	19,200					0	19,200
95	19,200					0	19,200
96	19,200					0	19,200
97	19,200					0	19,200
98	19,200					0	19,200

NOTES

Introduction

1. Andrew Jackson, quoted in E. J. Dionne, *Our Divided Political Heart* (New York: Bloomsbury, 2012), 179–180.

2. Wikipedia, s. v. "Sutton's Law," last modified January 29, 2017, www.wikipedia.org /wiki/Sutton%27s_law.

Chapter 1: The Emergence of an American Nation

1. Colin Woodard, *American Nations: A History of the Eleven Rival Regional Cultures of North America* (New York: Penguin Books, 2012), 5; 57–64.

2. Woodard, *American Nations*, 65–72.

3. Woodard, *American Nations*, 6–7.

4. Woodard, *American Nations*, 7; 44–54.

5. Woodard, *American Nations*, 8.

6. Woodard, *American Nations*, 9; 82–85.

7. Joseph J. Ellis, *The Quartet: Orchestrating the Second American Revolution, 1783–1789* (New York: Alfred A. Knopf, 2015), xi; xii; xiii; 6; 16.

8. Woodward, *American Nations*, 123–125.

9. Ellis, *The Quartet*, 16–19.

10. Wikipedia, s. v. "Battles of Saratoga," last modified August 2, 2018, www.wikipedia.org/wiki/Battles_of_Saratoga #Second_Saratoga:_Battle_of_Bemis_Heights_(October_7).

11. Wikipedia, s. v. "Siege of Yorktown," last modified August 16, 2018, www.wikipedia .org/wiki/Siege_of_Yorktown.

12. George Washington, quoted in Joseph J. Ellis, *The Quartet: Orchestrating the Second American Revolution, 1783–1789* (New York: Alfred A. Knopf, 2015), 60.

13. Ellis, *The Quartet*, 26–28.

14. Ellis, *The Quartet*, 128.

15. Ellis, *The Quartet*, 144.

16. Ellis, *The Quartet*, 148–149.

17. Wikiquote, s. v. "Abraham Lincoln," last modified August 17, 2018, www.wikiquote .org/wiki/Abraham_Lincoln.

Chapter 2: Interpreting the Law

1. *"Dred Scott v. Sandford,"* Oyez, www.oyez.org/cases/1850-1900/60us393.

2. Wikipedia, s. v. *"United States v. Cruikshank,"* last modified July 27, 2018, www.wikipedia.org/wiki/United_States_v._Cruikshank.

3. *"Plessy v. Ferguson,"* 163 US 537, 548 (1896).

4. *"Wong Wing v. United States,"* Oyez, www.oyez.org/cases/1850-1900/163us228.

5. Wikipedia, s. v. "Scott Act (1888)," last modified June 27, 2017, https://en.wikipedia.org/wiki/Scott_Act_(1888).

6. Ian Millhiser, *Injustices: The Supreme Court's History of Comforting the Comfortable and Afflicting the Afflicted* (New York: Nation Books, 2015), 57.

7. Wikipedia, s. v. "Sherman Antitrust Act of 1890," last modified August 8, 2018, www.wikipedia.org/wiki/Sherman_Antitrust_Act.

8. *"Hammer v. Dagenhart,"* Oyez, www.oyez.org/cases/1900-1940/247us251.

9. *"Buck v. Bell,"* Oyez, www.oyez.org/cases/1900-1940/274us200.

10. Millhiser, *Injustices*, 134–145.

11. *"Korematsu v. United States,"* Oyez, www.oyez.org/cases/1940-1955/323us214.

12. Millhiser, *Injustices*, 214.

13. *"Citizens United v. Federal Election Committee,"* Oyez, https://www.oyez.org/cases/2008/08-205.

14. Millhiser, *Injustices*, 235.

15. John Paul Stevens, *Six Amendments: How and Why We Should Change the Constitution* (New York: Little, Brown, 2014), 132.

16. Cass R. Sunstein, "The Most Mysterious Right," *The New Republic*, November 17, 2007, www.newrepublic.com/article/76368/second-amendment-gun-rights.

17. Jonathan Masters, "U.S. Gun Policy: Global Comparisons," Council on Foreign Relations, updated November 14, 2017, www.cfr.org/backgrounder/us-gun-policy-global-comparisons.

18. Christopher S. Koper, "Updated Assessment of the Federal Assault Weapons Ban," June 2004, www.ncjrs.gov/App/Publications/abstract.aspx?ID=204431.

19. Tom McCarthy, Lois Beckett, and Jessica Glenza, "America's Passion for Guns: Ownership and Violence by the Numbers," *Guardian*, October 3, 2017, https://www.theguardian.com/us-news/2017/oct/02/us-gun-control-ownership-violence-statistics.

20. Helena Bachman, "The Swiss Difference: A Gun Culture That Works," *Time*, December 20, 2012, http://world.time.com/2012/12/20/the-swiss-difference-a-gun-culture-that-works/.

21. "Extract from Thomas Jefferson to H. Tompkinson (Samuel Kercheval)," The Jefferson Monticello, http://tjrs.monticello.org/letter/1384.

22. Dionne, *Our Divided Political Heart*, 135.

Chapter 3: One Citizen, One Vote

1. Wikipedia, s. v. "Federalist No. 68," August 4, 2018, www.wikipedia.org/wiki/Federalist_No._68.

2. Joel K. Goldstein, "Electoral College," American Bar Association, Division for Public Education, 1996, www.americanbar.org/content/dam/aba/migrated/publiced/lawday/schools/lessons/pdfs/electoralcollege.authcheckdam.pdf.

3. Wikipedia, s. v. "List of U.S. States by Historical Population," last modified August 16, 2018, www.wikipedia.org/wiki/List_of_U.S._states_by_historical_population.

4. Wikipedia, s. v. "List of U.S. States and Territories by Population," last modified August 6, 2018, www.wikipedia.org/wiki/List_of_U.S._states_and_territories_by_population.

5. David Leip, "2016 Presidential General Election Results," US Election Atlas, www.uselectionatlas.org/RESULTS/index.html.

6. Stevens, *Six Amendments*, 53.

7. Thom File, *Young-Adult Voting: An Analysis of Presidential Elections, 1964–2012* (Washington, DC: United States Census Bureau, 2014), www.census.gov/prod/2014pubs/p20-573.pdf.

8. Millhiser, *Injustices*, 219–224.

9. Stevens, *Six Amendments*, 34.

10. Millhiser, *Injustices*, 219–224.

Chapter 4: A Universal Safety Net

1. Ivana Kottasova, "Will Switzerland give every adult $2,500 a month?" CNN, May 24, 2016, www.money.cnn.com/2016/05/24/news/economy/switzerland-guaranteed-basic-income/index.html.

2. Charles Murray, *Guaranteed Income as a Replacement for the Welfare State* (Oxford, UK: Foundation for Law, Justice and Society, n.d.), www.fljs.org/files/publications/Murray.pdf.

3. Robert B. Reich, *Saving Capitalism: For the Many, Not the Few* (New York: Alfred A. Knopf, 2015), 214.

4. Wikipedia, s. v. "Mincome," last modified July 20, 2018, www.wikipedia.org/wiki/Mincome.

5. Kathleen Ronayne, "Stockton Stipend Pilot Study," California Today, *New York Times*, July 11, 2018.

Chapter 5: Market-Based Universal Health Care

1. "Health-Care Reform: Prescription for the Future," *Economist*, April 8, 2017, 52.

2. T. R. Reid, *The Healing of America: A Global Quest for Better, Cheaper, and Fairer Health Care* (New York: Penguin Press, 2009), 31–34.

3. Reid, *Healing of America*, 227–228.

4. Reid, *Healing of America*, 10.

5. Reid, *Healing of America*, 11–12; 18.

6. Reid, *Healing of America*, 2; 149.

7. Reid, *Healing of America*, 34–35.

8. Reid, *Healing of America*, 37–39.

9. Reid, *Healing of America*, 41–43.

10. Reid, *Healing of America*, 57–60.

11. "NHE Fact Sheet," Centers for Medicare and Medicaid Services, last modified April 17, 2018, www.cms.gov/research-statistics-data-and-systems/statistics-trends-and-reports/nationalhealthexpenddata/nhe-fact-sheet.html.

12. David Goldhill, *Catastrophic Care: Why Everything We Think We Know about Health Care Is Wrong* (New York: Alfred A. Knopf, 2013), 66; 230.

13. "Doctors and Pharmacists: An Underused Resource to Manage Drug Costs for Older Adults," National Poll on Healthy Aging, University of Michigan, June 30, 2017, www.healthyagingpoll.org/report/julyaugust-2017-report-doctors-and-pharmacists-underused-drug-costs.

14. Goldhill, *Catastrophic Care*, 28–31.

15. "Nutrition, Physical Activity, and Obesity," National Center for Chronic Disease Prevention and Health Promotion, Centers for Disease Control and Prevention, last modified November 13, 2017, https://www.cdc.gov/chronicdisease/resources/publications/aag/dnpao.htm.

16. Goldhill, *Catastrophic Care*, 126.

17. Goldhill, *Catastrophic Care*, 147.

18. Goldhill, *Catastrophic Care*, 230–234.

19. Goldhill, *Catastrophic Care*, 23.

20. "Mending Mortality: End-of-Life Care," *Economist*, April 29, 2017, 45–48.

21. Kellie Scott, "Dying at Home More Peaceful than in Hospital and Better for Loved Ones, Research Finds," ABC News, October 10, 2015, www.abc.net.au/news/2015-10-11/dying-at-home-more-peaceful-than-in-hospital-study-finds/6844746.

Chapter 6: Educational Opportunity

1. Marisol Cuellar Mejia and Hans Johnson, "Higher College Attainment Will Raise wages but Not Narrow Income Gap," EdSource, April 23, 2014, www.edsource.org/2014/higher-college-attainment-will-raise-wages-but-not-narrow-income-gap/63535.

2. Joel Mokyr, "The Onrushing Wave," *Economist*, January 18, 2014, www.economist.com/briefing/2014/01/18/the-onrushing-wave.

3. "Active Labour Market Policies: Connecting People with Jobs," Organisation for Economic Co-operation and Development, www.oecd.org/employment /activation.htm.

4. "William James Talks to Teachers on Psychology," University of Kentucky, www.uky .edu/~eushe2/Pajares/talks1.html.

5. "The Assignment Process," San Francisco Public Schools, www.sfusd.edu /en/enroll-in-sfusd-schools/how-student-assignment-works/the-assignment -process.html.

6. "Must Try Harder," *Economist*, December 10, 2016, 59–61.

7. "George Washington < Quotes < Quotable Quote," Goodreads, www.goodreads .com/quotes/26168-a-primary-object-should-be-the-education-of-our-youth.

8. "Thomas Jefferson: Founding Father Quote," Founding Father Quotes, www .foundingfatherquotes.com/quote/713.

9. "James Madison Quotes," BrainyQuote, www.brainyquote.com/quotes /james_madison_383328.

10. "Five into Four," *Economist*, February 3, 2018, 27.

11. "Keeping the Wheels Turning," *Economist*, December 23, 2017, 39–40.

12. "To See Divide between Rich Schools and Poor, Look to Waukegan and Stevenson," *Chicago Tribune*, September 6, 2016, www.chicagotribune.com/ . . . /lake . . . /ct-rich-poor-school-districts-20160906-story.html.

13. Rebecca Mead, "The Lessons of Mayor Bill de Blasio's Universal Pre-K Initiative," *New Yorker*, September 7, 2017, www.newyorker.com/news/daily-comment /the-lessons-of-mayor-bill-de-blasios-universal-pre-k-initiative.

14. Allesandra Lanza, "Alternative to Student Loans: Income-Share Agreements," *U. S. News and World Report*, January 24, 2018, www. usnews.com/education/blogs/student-loan-ranger/articles/2018-01-24/ alternative-to-student-loans-income-share-agreements.

15. Michelle Ye Hee Lee, "Yes, U.S. Locks People Up at a Higher Rate than Any Other Country," *Washington Post*, July 7, 2015, www.washingtonpost.com/news/fact -checker/wp/2015/07/07/yes-u-s-locks-people-up-at-a-higher-rate-than-any -other-country/?utm_term=.875869701160.

Chapter 7: National Defense

1. Dave Mosher and Skye Gould, "How Likely Are Foreign Terrorists to Kill Americans? The Odds May Surprise You," Business Insider, January 31, 2017, www .businessinsider.com/death-risk-statistics-terrorism-disease-accidents-2017-1.

2. Wikipedia, s. v. "Rikki-Tikki-Tavi," last modified August 13, 2018, www.wikipedia .org/wiki/Rikki-Tikki-Tavi.

3. Ronen Bergman, *Rise and Kill First: The Secret History of Israel's Targeted Assassinations* (New York: Random House, 2018).

4. David Francis, "How North Korea Starved Its People for a Nuke," *Fiscal Times*, April 9, 2013, www.thefiscaltimes.com/Articles/2013/04/09 /How-North-Korea-Starved-Its-People-for-a-Nuke.

5. "Welcome to the Wingbot," *Economist*, July 7, 2018, 64–65.

6. Darren Orf, "The New Zumwalt Stealth Destroyer Is *Too* Stealthy," Gizmodo, April 12, 2016, www.gizmodo.com/the-new-zumwalt-stealth-destroyer-is-too -stealthy-1770458856.

7. John Mangels, "Blending the Best of Helicopters and Airplanes, the MV-22 Osprey Tiltrotor Shows Its Stuff during Marine Week in Cleveland," Cleveland.com, June 13, 2012, www.cleveland.com/science/index.ssf/2012/06/blending_the_best_of _helicopte.html.

8. Rich Smith, "Textron's New Drone Is a Game Changer," The Motley Fool, October 8, 2016, www.fool.com/investing/2016/10/08/textrons-new-drone-is-a-game -changer.aspx.

9. Sydney J. Freedberg Jr., "Army $40B Short on Modernization vs. Russia, China: CSA Milley," Breaking Defense, October 3, 2016, BreakingDefense.com/2016/10 /army-40b-short-on-modernization-vs-russia-china-csa-milley/

10. "The New Battlegrounds," *Economist*, February 27, 2018, 3–4; 8–12; 15–16.

11. Jeremy Bender, "This Map Shows How Many More Military Aircraft the US Has Than Every Other Country on Earth," Business Insider, January 28, 2015, www .businessinsider.com/military-aircraft-strength-of-every-country-2015-1.

Chapter 8: Taxation and Resource Allocation

1. "Under Audit," *Economist*, April 29, 2017, 10.

2. "Federal Spending: Where Does the Money Go," National Priorities Project, https://www.nationalpriorities.org/budget-basics/federal-budget-101/spending/.

3. "Federal Revenue: Where Does the Money Come From," National Priorities Project, www.nationalpriorities.org/budget-basics/federal-budget-101/revenues/.

4. Organisation for Economic Co-operation and Development, *Revenue Statistics 2016*, Organisation for Economic Co-operation and Development, 2016, www .oecd.org/tax/tax-policy/revenue-statistics-2016-highlights.pdf.

5. Eric Jaffe, "America's Infrastructure Crisis Is Really a Maintenance Crisis," CityLab, February 12, 2015, www.citylab.com/solutions/2015/02 /americas-infrastructure-crisis-is-really-a-maintenance-crisis/385452/.

6. Rachel Tiede, "Clinton Correct Buffett Claimed to Pay a Lower Tax Rate than His Secretary," PolitiFact, October 18, 2016, www.politifact.com/truth-o-meter /statements/2016/oct/18/hillary-clinton/clinton-correct-buffett- claimed-pay-lower-tax-rate/.

7. Joseph E. Stiglitz, *Rewriting the Rules of the American Economy* (New York: W. W. Norton, 2016).

8. Reich, *Saving Capitalism*.

9. "Adam Smith Favored Progressive Taxation," Daily KOS, October 21, 2009, www
    .dailykos.com/stories/2009/10/21/795604/-.

10. "Friedrich A. Hayek < Quotes," Goodreads, www.goodreads.com/author/quotes
    /670307.Friedrich_A_Hayek.

11. William McBride, "A Brief History of Tax Expenditures," Tax Foundation, August
    22, 2013, www.taxfoundation.org/brief-history-tax-expenditures/.

12. "Distribution of Households in the United States from 1970 to 2017, by Household
    Size," Statista, www.statista.com/statistics/242189/disitribution-of-households
    -in-the-us-by-household-size/.

13. Matthew O'Brien, "Why the Mortgage Interest Deduction Is Terrible," *Atlantic*,
    July 17, 2012, www.theatlantic.com/business/archive/2012/07
    /why-the-mortgage-interest-deduction-is-terrible/259915/.

14. T. R. Reid, *A Fine Mess: A Global Quest for a Simpler, Fairer, and More Efficient Tax
    System* (New York: Penguin Press, 2017), 88–90.

15. Reid, *A Fine Mess*, 82–85.

16. Susan Dunn, "Teddy Roosevelt Betrayed," *New York Times*, August 9, 1999, www
    .nytimes.com/1999/08/09/opinion/teddy-roosevelt-betrayed.html.

17. James K. Glassman, "Inheritance and Sloth," *Forbes*, October 11, 1999, www.forbes
    .com/forbes/1999/1011/6409094a.html#4d83ed6b7732.

18. "The Case for Taxing Death," *Economist*, November 25, 2017, 13.

19. "The Corporate Tax Rate Debate: Lower Taxes on Corporate Profits Not Linked to
    Job Creation," Center for Effective Government, December 3, 2013, www
    .foreffectivegov.org/corp-tax-rate-debate.

20. "Value-Added Tax—VAT," Investopedia, www.investopedia.com/terms/v
    /valueaddedtax.asp.

21. Wikipedia, s. v. "Sin Tax," last modified August 9, 2018, www.wikipedia.org/wiki
    /Sin_tax.

22. James R. Hines, "Taxing Consumption and Other Sins," *Journal of Economic
    Perspectives* 21, no. 1 (2007): 49–68.

23. Joe Myers, "Which Countries Have the Highest Tax on Cigarettes?" World
    Economic Forum, May 4, 2016, www.weforum.org/agenda/2016/05
    /which-countries-have-the-highest-tax-on-cigarettes/.

24. Reid, *A Fine Mess*, 176.

25. "Ravenously Hungary: Obesity," *Economist*, June 10, 2017, 52.

26. Wikipedia, s. v. *Capital in the Twenty-First Century*," last modified July 5, 2018,
    www.wikipedia.org/wiki/Capital in the Twenty-First Century.

27. Leonard E. Burman and William G. Gale, "A Golden Opportunity to Simplify
    the Tax System: Options for Reforming a Complex Tax Code," Brookings, April 3,
    2001, www.brookings.edu/research/a-golden-opportunity-to-simplify-the-tax
    -system-options-for-reforming-a-complex-tax-code/.

28. "How Could We Improve the Federal Tax System?" Tax Policy Center, www
    .taxpolicycenter.org/briefing-book/what-are-ten-ways-simplify-tax-system.

29.   Cass R. Sunstein, "How to Simplify the Tax Code. Simply," *Time*, May 31, 2013, www.ideas.time.com/2013/05/31/how-to-simplify-the-tax-code-simply/.

Chapter 9: Government Regulations

1.   Stiglitz, cover to *Rewriting the Rules*.

2.   Schumpeter, "Crony Capitalism," *Economist*, April 15, 2017, 59.

3.   Committee for Economic Development, *Crony Capitalism: Unhealthy Relations Between Business and Government* (Arlington, VA: Committee for Economic Development, 2015), www.ced.org/pdf/CED_-_Crony_Capitalism_-_Report.pdf.

4.   Thomas R. Oliver, Philip R. Lee, and Helene L. Lipton, "A Political History of Medicare and Prescription Drug Coverage," *Milbank Quarterly* 82, no. 2 (June 2004), www.ncbi.nlm.nih.gov/pmc/articles/PMC2690175/.

5.   Hannah Yi, "This Is How Internet Speed and Price in the U.S. Compares to the Rest of the World," PBS News Hour, April 26, 2015, www.pbs.org/newshour /world/internet-u-s-compare-globally-hint-slower-expensive.

6.   Vicki Needham, "House Bill Cuts IRS Funding," The Hill, May 24, 2016, www .thehill.com/policy/finance/appropriations/281052-house-bill-cuts-irs-funding.

7.   Richard Briffault, "Lobbying and Campaign Finance: Separate and Together," *Stanford Law and Policy Review* 19, no. 1 (2008): 105–129, web.stanford.edu/group /slpr/previous/Volume19/Briffault_19slpr105.pdf.

8.   John Nichols, "Teddy Roosevelt Was Right: Ban All Corporate Contributions," *The Nation*, January 21, 2010, www.thenation.com/article /teddy-roosevelt-was-right-ban-all-corporate-contributions/.

Chapter 10: Rejecting Partisan Tribalism

1.   Mickey Edwards, *The Parties versus the People: How to Turn Republicans and Democrats into Americans* (New Haven: Yale University Press, 2012), 3–32.

2.   Jeffrey M. Jones, "Democratic Party Maintains Edge in Party Affiliation," Gallup, December 4, 2017, news.gallup.com/poll/223124/democratic-party-maintains -edge-party-affiliation.aspx.

3.   "*Citizens United v. Federal Election Commission*," Oyez, www.oyez.org /cases/2008/08-205.

4.   "Ten Critiques (and Defenses) on Approval Voting," The Center for Election Science, October 31, 2017, www.electology.org/blog /ten-critiques-and-defenses-approval-voting.

5.   Jack Beatty, "A Sisyphean History of Campaign Finance Reform," *Atlantic*, July 2007, www.theatlantic.com/magazine/archive/2007/07/a-sisyphean-history-of -campaign-finance-reform/306066/.

Chapter 11: Two Americas

1. David Leip, "2016 Presidential General Election Results," US Election Atlas, www
.uselectionatlas.org/RESULTS/index.html.

2. David Roberts, "Your Vote in the 2016 Election Explains Almost Everything about
Your Climate Beliefs," Vox, last updated April 29, 2017, www.vox.com
/science-and-health/2017/3/23/15032488/climate-beliefs-2016-election-votes.

3. "American Democracy's Built-In Bias," *Economist*, July 14, 2018, 11.

4. "Counting Double," *Economist*, May 13, 2017, 9.

5. John Tierney, "Which States Are Givers and Which Are Takers?" *Atlantic*, May 5,
2014, www.theatlantic.com/business/archive/2014/05
/which-states-are-givers-and-which-are-takers/361668/.

6. Mark Muro and Sifan Liu, "Another Clinton-Trump Divide: High-Output
America vs Low-Output America," Brookings, November 29, 2016, www.brookings
.edu/blog/the-avenue/2016/11/29/another-clinton-trump-divide-high-output
-america-vs-low-output-america/.

Chapter 12: Facing Reality

1. David J. Lynch, Josh Dawsey, and Damian Paletta, "Trump imposes steel and
aluminum tariffs on the E.U., Canada and Mexico," *Washington Post*, May 31, 2018,
www.washingtonpost.com/business/economy/trump-imposes-steel-and-aluminum
-tariffs-on-the-european-union-canada-and-mexico/2018/05/31/891bb452-64d3-
11e8-a69c-b944de66d9e7_story.html?utm_term=.178caf47d7b3.

2. "Roaring Away: Harley-Davidson Shifts Production," *Economist*, June 30, 2018, 61.

3. "The Value of U.S. Energy Exports to Mexico Exceeded Import Value for Third Year
in a Row," U.S. Energy Information Administration, March 14, 2018, www.eia.gov
/todayinenergy/detail.php?id=35332.

4. Richard Partington, "IMF Warns Trump Trade War Could Cost Global Economy
$430bn," *Guardian*, July 16, 2018, www.theguardian.com/business/2018/jul/16
/imf-trump-trade-war-global-economy-us-tariff-weo.

5. Steven Rattner, "Trump's Chaos Theory: A Single Tweet Causes Jobs to Return,"
New York Times, December 1, 2016, www.nytimes.com/2016/12/01/opinion
/trumps-chaos-theory-a-single-tweet-causes-jobs-to-return.html.

6. "The Factories of the Future," *Economist*, July 1, 2017, 19–22.

7. "US Agricultural Exports to Mexico and Canada Amounted to $41 Billion in
2016," Quartz Index, July 17, 2017, www.index.qz.com/1030013/nafta-the-us
-exported-more-than-40-billion-in-farm-products-to-mexico-and-canada-trump
-might-change-that/.

8. James R. Nunns, Leonard E. Burman, Jeffrey Rohaly, and Joseph Rosenberg, "An
Analysis of Donald Trump's Revised Tax Plan," Tax Policy Center, October 18, 2016,
www.taxpolicycenter.org/publications/analysis-donald-trumps-revised-tax-plan.

9. "Employment and Wages," *Economist*, July 14, 2018, 25–26.

10. Michael Rainey, "The Steep Costs of Tax Cuts Since 2001," *The Fiscal Times*, July 11, 2018, www.thefiscaltimes.com/2018/07/11/Steep-Costs-Tax-Cuts-2001.

11. Robert C. Pozen, "Donald Trump's Tax Plan Could Land America $10 Trillion Deeper in Debt," Brookings, March 7, 2016, www.brookings.edu/opinions /donald-trumps-tax-plan-could-land-america-10-trillion-deeper-in-debt/.

12. Noah Lanard, "Economists Think Republicans' Tax Numbers Are a Joke," *Mother Jones*, September 29, 2017, www.motherjones.com/kevin-drum/2017/09 /economists-think-republicans-tax-numbers-are-a-joke/.

13. Nicole Goodkind, "Trump Tax Plan: 80 Percent of Economic Gains Will End Up Going to Foreigners in 2028, Democratic Senator Says," *Newsweek*, April 12, 2018, www.newsweek.com/republican-tax-plan-donald-trump-cbo-884129.

14. Nicole Goodkind, "Trump's Tax Cuts Didn't Benefit U.S. Workers, Made Rich Companies Richer, Analysis Finds," *Newsweek*, April 10, 2018, www.newsweek.com /republican-tax-cuts-trump-wage-increases-879800.

15. "Redistribution: For Richer, For Poorer," *Economist*, November 25, 2017, 23–24.

16. Eleanor Ainge Roy, "Work Less, Get More: New Zealand Firm's Four-Day Week an 'Unmitigated Success,'" *Guardian*, July 18, 2018, https://www.theguardian.com/world/2018/jul/19/ work-less-get-more-new-zealand-firms-four-day-week-an-unmitigated-success.

17. Daniel Kahneman, *Thinking, Fast and Slow* (New York: Farrar, Straus and Giroux, 2011).

Chapter 13: Clean-Energy Technology

1. "Hollar Promises: Coal," *Economist*, December 16, 2017, 26–27.

2. Brian Wang, "A Copper Oxide Solar Cells on Top of Regular Silicon Solar Cells Could Boost Energy Conversion up to 40% from 25% Today," Next Big Future, March 29, 2017, www.nextbigfuture.com/2017/03/a-copper-oxide-solar-cells-on -top-of.html.

3. David Roberts, "These Huge New Wind Turbines Are a Marvel. They're Also the Future," Vox, April 13, 2018, www.vox.com/ energy-and-environment/2018/3/8/17084158/wind-turbine-power-energy-blades.

4. Alexander C. Kaufman, "Wind to Blow Past Hydropower as Top Clean Electricity Source in Major Milestone," *HuffPost*, January 24, 2018, www.huffingtonpost.com /entry/wind-energy-eia_us_5a68bae7e4b002283008b3b7.

5. "Solar Energy: Helios's Crystal," *Economist*, February 3, 2018, 67–68.

6. "China's Embrace of a New Electricity-Transmission Technology Holds Lessons for Others," *Economist*, January 14, 2017, www.economist.com/leaders/2017/01/14 /chinas-embrace-of-a-new-electricity-transmission-technology-holds-lessons-for -others.

7. Ryan Whitman, "Samsung: Graphene Balls Boost Battery Charging Speed by 500 Percent," Extreme Tech, December 1, 2017, www.extremetech.com /extreme/259772-graphene-balls-boost-battery-capacity-45-charging-speed-500.

8. Brian Wang, "Graphene Oxide Supercapacitor on Verge of Commercialization," Next Big Future, June 16, 2017, www.nextbigfuture.com/2017/06/graphene-oxide -supercapacitor-on-verge-of-commercialization.html.

9. Julie Chao, "'Holy Grail' for Batteries: Solid-State Magnesium Battery a Big Step Closer," Berkeley Lab, November 28, 2017, https://newscenter.lbl.gov/2017/11/28 /holy-grail-batteries-solid-state-magnesium-battery-big-step-closer/.

10. Henry S. Kenyon, "A Clear Winner in Charge to Build Better Batteries," SIGNAL, July 1, 2017, www.afcea.org/content/Article-clear-winner-charge-build -better-batteries.

11. William Pentland, "German Utility Plans to Build World's Biggest Battery in a Salt Cavern," Forbes, June 30, 2017, www.forbes.com/sites/williampentland/2017/06/30 /german-utility-plans-to-build-worlds-biggest-battery-in-a-salt- cavern/#414976ee7feb.

12. Jon Fingas, "Liquid Metal Battery Could Lower Cost of Storing Renewable Energy," Engadget, July 23, 2018, https://www.engadget.com/2018/07/23 /liquid-metal-battery-could-lower-cost-of-storing-renewable-energ/.

13. Leslie Shaffer, "Electric Vehicles Will Soon Be Cheaper Than Regular Cars because Maintenance Costs Are Lower, Says Tony Seba," CNBC, June 14, 2016, www.cnbc .com/2016/06/14/electric-vehicles-will-soon-be-cheaper-than-regular-cars-because -maintenance-costs-are-lower-says-tony-seba.html.

14. "Let's Twist Again: Electric Motors," Economist, September 16, 2017, 73.

15. David Brown, "Nuclear Power Is Safest Way to Make Electricity, According to Study," Washington Post, April 2, 2011, www.washingtonpost.com/national/nuclear -power-is-safest-way-to-make-electricity-according-to-2007-study/2011/03/22 /AFQUbyQC_story.html?utm_term=.50cc1136222a.

16. Clayton Sandell, "What's in a Number? New Carbon Dioxide Level Unseen in Human History," ABC News, May 10, 2013, abcnews.go.com/Technology /carbon-dioxide-level-unseen-human-history/story?id=19152850.

17. "As Seas Rise, NASA Zeros In: How Much? How Fast?" NASA, last updated August 3, 2017, www.nasa.gov/goddard/risingseas.

18. Hannah Ritchie and Max Roser, "Air Pollution," Our World in Data, last updated October 2017, www.ourworldindata.org/air-pollution.

Chapter 14: Enhancing Genetic Inheritance

1. "Watson and Crick Discover Chemical Structure of DNA," History, www.history .com/this-day-in-history/watson-and-crick-discover-chemical-structure-of-dna.

2. "Using DNA to Predict Schizophrenia and Autism," Science Daily, August 30, 2017, www.sciencedaily.com/releases/2017/08/170830094309.htm.

3. Aparna Vidyasagar, "What is CRISPR?" Live Science, April 20, 2018, www .livescience.com/58790-crispr-explained.html.

4. Marcel Adam Just et al., "Mental Rotation of Objects Retrieved from Memory," Journal of Experimental Psychology: General 130, no. 3 (2001): 493–504.

Chapter 15: A Comprehensive Plan

1. Schumpeter, "Political Business," *Economist*, November 5, 2016, www.economist
   .com/business/2016/11/05/political-business.

2. Emmanuel Saez, "U.S. Top One Percent of Income Earners Hit New High in 2015
   amid Strong Economic Growth," Washington Center for Equitable Growth, July 1,
   2016, www.equitablegrowth.org/u-s-top-one-percent-of-income-earners-hit-new
   -high-in-2015-amid-strong-economic-growth/.

3. "Democracy in America Quotes," Goodreads, www.goodreads.com/work
   /quotes/90454-de-la-d-mocratie-en-am-rique.

4. "The Worst Form of Government," The International Churchill Society, www
   .winstonchurchill.org/resources/quotes/the-worst-form-of-government/.

5. Dionne, *Our Divided Political Heart*, 256.

6. Dionne, *Our Divided Political Heart*, 70–71.

7. Dionne, *Our Divided Political Heart*, 91.

8. Dionne, *Our Divided Political Heart*, 132.

9. "The Minority Majority," *Economist*, July 14, 2018, 21.

10. "The Minority Majority," 24.

11. "Science Makes Progress Funeral by Funeral," Quote Investigator, September 25,
    2017, www.quoteinvestigator.com/2017/09/25/progress/.

ABOUT THE AUTHOR

Peter W. Frey is a research scientist whose experience covers a wide range of disciplines and interests. He is a professor emeritus at Northwestern University, where he served on the faculty for thirty years, teaching in the computer science department, the psychology department, and the Kellogg Graduate School of Management. While at Northwestern, his research focused on machine learning and computer-based decision systems. He is the author of over sixty academic publications and several commercial software products. In recent years, he managed a small technology company that pioneered commercial applications in predictive analytics. Peter graduated magna cum laude from Yale University and earned his PhD in experimental psychology from the University of Wisconsin.

Peter enjoys outdoor activities, including hiking, mountain climbing, road biking, and stone masonry. In his early sixties, he acquired a staph infection from cuts he received while landscaping his property. The infection that settled in his lower spinal cord was almost fatal—he was paralyzed from the waist down for over a month. He began working out on a three-wheel recumbent road bike to rebuild his legs and slowly gained lower body strength. These workouts led to him ultimately participating in three Ride the Rockies cross-country tours that involved daily, 80-mile rides with multiple climbs over mountain passes exceeding 12,000 feet in elevation. He cites those workouts as being his salvation and the reason he continues to enjoy an active outdoor lifestyle. Every morning, he gets up knowing that each day is a precious gift.

INDEX